If you are having trouble getting your students engaged in language arts activities this is the book for you. It is chock full of well-explained and simple teaching strategies that will help students learn how to write and read better and enjoy the process as well.

—Dr. Betty Jane Wagner, professor, College of Education, Roosevelt University (nationally known educator and educational author, co-wrote with internationally known educator/researcher James Moffett). Author of *Student-Centered Language Arts, K-12* (and many other books).

This important book is a must-read for anyone who teaches language arts from grade four and up. James Charnock possesses one of the most creative and inspiring voices emerging from the language pedagogy community today. While often challenging traditional teaching methods, he brings his thirty years of teaching experience and his generous heart to offer a wide range of practical, fun, and well-detailed strategies to teaching language arts. His unusual, exuberant, student-centered techniques meet the child in his/her own world and go on to open up new dimensions of experience and mastery of language skills. Here is a treasury of specific directions, charts, forms, lists, scales, and games, often with engaging titles, for drawing the student into the learning experience. Samples of students' responses reflect the rewarding outcomes that so often have validated this teacher's dedication, love, and imaginative solutions to the challenge of teaching language arts. This compilation of Charnock's work serves as a valuable resource to empower students with not only better language skills, but also with a better sense of self. His teaching methods can stimulate awareness and self-expression, which are among the most useful life skills a child can acquire.

—Wandz Costanzo, Ph.D., clinical psychologist (subspecialty: Attention Deficit Disorder), private practice, Haddonfield, New Jersey

James Charnock is someone whose personality has been created for me by his written words. Like Odysseus, he is the man never at a loss. I'd be willing to bet that in his school students [fought] to get into his classes, parents pulled whatever strings they could to get their kids in, and colleagues benefited from his innovative ideas, of which he seems to have a never-ending supply. Readers of the [Arizona English] Bulletin over the years have also benefited from his resourcefulness.

—Dr. Margaret B. Fleming, former editor,
Arizona English Bulletin
(Affiliate of the National Council of Teachers of English)

A Non-Workbook, Non-Textbook Approach to Teaching Language Arts

(Grades 4 through 8 and up)

James T. Charnock

Dr. Wagner, Thanks for the inspiration! Jim Charnock

A Non-Workbook, Non-Textbook Approach to Teaching Language Arts

Published by Fenestra Books™
610 East Delano Street, Suite 104, Tucson, Arizona 85705 U.S.A.
www.fenestrabooks.com
ISBN: 1-58736-521-9
LCCN: 2005929244

Acknowledgements

The inspiration for teaching writing and the language arts began early in my career when I read *Student-Centered Language Arts, K-12* by an internationally known pair of educators, James Moffett and Betty Jane Wagner. Dr. Wagner is a professor of education at Roosevelt University's College of Education and director of the Chicago Area Writing Project. Her co-written book—my language arts "bible"—is still very up-to-date and available at Heinemann Books (www.heinemann.com) in its fourth edition. Dr. Wagner and Jan Moffett gave permission to use one of the book's ideas, which I adapted into Chapter 2. Dr. Wagner also graciously read and endorsed this book.

Another great debt of gratitude willingly goes to the well-respected Haddonfield, New Jersey, clinical psychologist, Dr. Wandz Costanzo, who pored over the manuscript and gave a rousing thumbs up to the approaches herein.

The *Arizona English Bulletin* (affiliated with the National Council of Teachers of English) is pleased that the ideas of some of my articles are being included: Chapters 6, 7, 8, 12, and 13. Dr. Margaret Fleming, former *Arizona* editor, just by her continual acceptance, encouraged me to share what I was learning in the classroom by teaching. I was always grateful. The NCTE granted permission of my adaptation of some of their material used in Chapters 5 and 16.

Teacher Magazine (which absorbed *Instructor Magazine*) granted use of the articles that became Chapters 1 and 4. I am also grateful to Birute Gudauskas, a Philadelphia teacher, who co-wrote and gave permission for Chapter 4; her initial task inspired me to add to her creation.

In Chapter 8 is the poem "The Lurpp is on the Loose;" text copyright © 1977 by Jack Prelutsky and used by permission of HarperCollins Publishers.

Chapter 11, adapted from another article of mine, is courtesy of *The Reading Teacher*, journal of the International Reading Association.

The other five chapters were newly composed for this book. Nevertheless, the last chapter, 16, is one of my favorites and the culmination of previous ideas. For many of the ideas in this chapter (the "Experts" approach) I owe a big thank-you to Franklin J. Chrisco, a fellow educator who resides in Brattleboro, Vermont.

Table of Contents

Paragraphing Made Simple

Learning paragraphing from trade or textbooks is about as appetizing as chewing leather. They are not engaging, not intellectually stimulating (that's their stated purpose, I believe), and, to some extent, not even correct. Teachers stand up and clap at seminars after experiencing this approach to paragraphing. You can simply enjoy the ideas and pass them on to your students. (Grades 5-12)

"Memory Writing": A Powerful Method for Teaching Paragraphing and Compositions—A Step-by-Step Approach

"Memory writing" is simple, engaging, very logical, and very elementary, my dear teacher. But it's only elementary because it's basic, and it's a wonderful starting, and continuing, point—not just for creative and expository compositions, but research as well. (Grades 5-12)

Teaching Book Reports? Do it right

They've been done for decades and will be for decades more. This chapter gives both teacher and student *examples*—from "fanciful fiction" to "minority" book reports. Includes book lists and a "Thumbs Up, Thumbs Down" student-rating chart. (Grades 4-12)

Letter Writing: Don't Let It Become a Lost Art
Computer or not, letter-writing skills and formats have to be learned. Here are sometimes-silly, reproducible assignments: concrete, simple, and short—a real time-saver for the teacher. (Grades 4-8)

Classroom Interviewing
Sounds easy enough, but there's a technique to such things, you know. Provides an example of two types of interviewing. Students will love the social interaction, too. (Grades 4-12)

The Art of Story*taking*
You can teach it 'til the cows come home, but unless you let the students get out in "the field" and practice, all those writing rules will take longer to sink in—and bore the students to boot. This program allows your class to enjoy all that English mechanics "stuff" you've been teaching. Milk it for all it's worth. (Grades 5-9)

LINE UP! —A Game, Not a Command
You would never guess from the title that this is an activity with capitalization and punctuation. No one else has it, and publishers have refused to publish it because "teachers will find it too easy to copy," as one put it. It's physically, socially, and intellectually exciting and just plain English-reinforcement fun. Close the door! (Grades 3/4-8)

"Doing" a Poem (Or How to Start Losing Your Fear of Classroom Drama)

Why let the class clown get all the attention? Here's an engaging drama-like activity that allows the whole class to participate in one way or another: choral speaking, a cappella singing (unless you play an instrument), art work, drama, and being a VIP or star to primary grade students. It's really English, but we won't tell them that. (Grades 4-6)

Diary Writing: I Hate It … I Love It

This is not one of those "you ought to do this, but I'm not going to lead you by the hand" chapters. I tell you *what* diary writing really is, *why* it is important, *how* to conduct your program—and give a list of intriguing topics to use in a pinch. (Grades 4-12)

Assisted Reading: When Children Aren't Learning Any Other Way

You've worked very diligently to help Johnny or Mary to read, but they are getting far behind and nothing seems to work. Barring any emotional, visual, or neurological impairment, why not try an approach you may not have thought of? (Grades 3-8)

Phonics and Syllables in the Middle and Upper Grades— Another Approach

If you have to teach any middle or upper elementary students who are really *primary* students, skill-wise, you need a shortcut to getting phonetic and word attack skills across. Check out these unusual, non-traditional, yet effective ideas. (Grades 4-8)

Killing Three Birds with One Stone (Or Using Picture Books to Improve the Mechanics of Public Speaking and Overcome Stage Fright in Middle, Junior, and High School Students)

Get those students out of their seats and performing in other classrooms! This easy-to-follow program not only engenders student excitement (yes, they're fearful, at first), but teaches the maturing public speaking and anti-stage-fright skills every child and adult should possess. (Grades 4-12)

How to Gain a Reputation

Students sometimes can't decide on a good book to read, and sometimes teachers can't help them. This chapter helps you to expand your repertoire of good books to suggest. A colorful book-rating chart is provided for posting.

A Mini-Potpourri of Ideas to Spark Structured Creativity

Sometimes creativity does have a way of getting out of hand—especially in children. So, herein, you'll get fun ideas off the beaten path that yet allow you to know the students are enjoying *and* learning. (Grades 4-up)

Fun with Vocabulary

You know, of course, that vocabulary is supposedly a measure of intelligence. Then, there's the Miller Analogies Test, a claimed predictor of college success. Well, all that aside, just get those future writers into the fun of words. Writers have to have that. Here are two ways—including a free classroom game worth the price of this book alone! (Grades 2-8+)

Assaying the Essay
Say that again? Yes, there is a value to writing longer compositions. But just like money, it should not become onerous (well, maybe that is not a good analogy). The best past writers have admitted, and current ones do too, that they had mentors, examples to follow. And, dear teacher, you have the privilege of following in their successful steps: more student-written examples, less pedagogical falderal. (grades 5-up)

Experts: Becoming a True Researcher
Even that little brat of a kid torturing an ant is doing some research: He has questions, has formed a hypothesis, is testing it, and is finding a conclusion. This best-I've-ever-used approach for research projects is admittedly more erudite—even more fun. And it's easier than you might think. (Grades 5-12)

Introduction

Here are most of the school report-card subjects taught by the middle and upper grades: reading, math, science, history and/or social studies, English, health and/or sex education, spelling (yes, as a separate subject), and geography (likewise, often a separate subject)—and some schools will have a couple more. Every one of these comes with a text and a workbook. But imagine the following schedule that too many teachers put their students through on a daily basis:

"Take out your reading book and …"

"Now, take out your science text …"

"Put your spelling workbook on your desk …"

"Next, is social studies. Open up your book to …

Thank goodness for gym and art. No textbooks; no workbooks! (Well, some teachers even manage to monotonously "teach" art by-the-book, too.) A whole book could be written about the over-reliance on such aids to teaching by those unskilled in a particular subject—or, alas, subjects. Luckily, the area of English/language arts easily lends itself to something better.

Admittedly, educators are usually better at teaching one subject than another, but the wholesale use of texts and workbooks is inexcusable, dulling to the mind, non-socially-interactive, and basically ineffective—for both the students and teacher. This *non*-textbook allows you no more excuses to rely on such lock-step aids in order to teach the skills covered herein.

I have examined many texts and workbooks (some faddishly modernized as "e-books" to download from the Internet) and found that less than ten percent of the material is even moderately useful. And not just from a pedagogical point of view, but also taking into consideration the students' physical, emotional, and social needs when learning.

Hopefully, the above percentage can be reversed and you will find ninety percent of the ideas contained in this non-textbook, non-workbook resource useful, even exciting. You will also feel a sense of freedom.

A Secret to Writing

Both you and I may not give much thought to *how* we write because what we have learned is such a part of us now. Yet, we know other "educated" people who are terrible writers. They have difficulty in sequencing ideas, opening and closing a composition, their writing suffers from a lack of clarity and is riddled with verbosity, they have no discernable style (admittedly a very subjective term to some), and others seem to have spent little time studying grammar and spelling.

Can we do something about the above faults? Maybe not. Many of these people sat in the same classes as those who can churn out endearing, absorbing, humorous, clear and serious articles and books.

I will state two things that I have found (and read of) to be obvious. If a child or adult reads a lot and writes a lot, he or she will probably do rather well at writing even if writing is not a favorite past time.

Because I have always subscribed to the above, I as a teacher, have always insisted that my students write daily, read for 30 minutes every day, and that they listen to literature ("story time") for 20-30 minutes every day. They *have* to experience language. And this zest for language needs to spill over into having fun with words/vocabulary development. Research has been done that backs up this philosophy.

So, one way to get your students on the road to better writing and speaking is to make them (and I mean with interest) read, write and listen to various types of literature.

Finally, I will acknowledge a philosophy I put into effect in this book. I have purposely left off dates. If a book, technique, or idea is good, it is good. Period. We still enjoy books and ideas by Twain, Tolstoy, Tolkien, Faulkner, Shakespeare, and others. The ideas herein have been thoroughly classroom tested by me and others—which takes time. So, enjoy their very current value.

Chapter 1

Paragraphing Made Simple

*Paragraphs are a story's basic unit—
like innings in a baseball game.*

Although I've done much writing myself, it took me some time to acquire a satisfactory technique for teaching children specific organizational skills. And I had trouble finding textbooks and curriculum guides with helpful ideas. So, I decided that it was up to me to develop an approach to teaching my students the basic structural unit of both imaginative and more practical types of writing—the paragraph. But how?

The simple had eluded me. Introducing paragraphing is really as easy as teaching any other subject. Like most, it can be approached both inductively, by "building" a paragraph or passage, and deductively, by analyzing an existing paragraph. Since the inductive process lends itself more readily to original compositions, I decided to concentrate on this approach, at least initially. I also decided to emphasize the children's ability to paragraph rather than the quality of their compositions.

Practice with paragraphing builds a good foundation for writing skills, whether the student is a third grader or in high school. Some of my paragraphing techniques not only foster original composition and thinking, but also indirectly teach outlining and researching skills. They help the student both organize a whole topic as well as write individual paragraphs. And the skills learned are transferable to any curriculum area.

The Main Events

For our first paragraphing venture, I chose a topic with which the children would be familiar and that could be readily broken down into recognizable units of time—"Today's Class Periods." Other suitable topics include "Events of the Weekend," "Seasons," and "Events of a Story." I listed the subject areas in order on the board—reading, math, gym, recess, etc.—and, starting at the top of the list, asked the children to relate the main events of and their feelings about each period. As the students commented, I recorded their remarks in abbreviated form on the chalkboard.

When we had gone through the list, I talked to the class about the first period, including only the remarks listed on the board. Then I asked for volunteers to talk about the remaining periods in the same manner. I helped the children with transitional sentences for each class period.

In the next session, I wrote the events of another morning on the board, based on the children's contributions. This time I transformed comments about the first period into a written paragraph:

Our first activity is reading. During the first part of the period, Mr. Charnock teaches the whole class. Then we work by ourselves or in groups. We have assignments we must finish before the week is over. We can play an educational game any day we can show we are not behind in our work.

Next, I directed the students to write about the other periods, making sure they indented for each new period's "paragraph." When they finished, I asked the students what they thought was the reason for paragraphing. Their response was as expected: "Each paragraph is about a different period or subject." To reinforce this generalization, we later followed the same procedure with the events of a favorite story.

Play Ball!

My initial approach had been mainly chronological. I also wanted the students to be able to outline their writing from a more topical viewpoint. I informed the students that we were going to be concerned with an interesting topic of their choice and asked for a few one-word title suggestions. (I wrote "arithmetic" on the board, but few voted for it.) Among the topics suggested were "holidays," "superstitions," and "war." Finally, they selected "baseball." I asked the students to name up to twenty things they thought were important about this topic, and I listed the words on the board in the order given.

Step 1 (Listing):

bat, catcher, runs, outs, shortstop, bases, glove, field, strikes, fun, arguing, fouls, fielder, pitcher, exercise, winning, losing, innings

---

Then I asked the class to group the words that seemed to go together. There was some disagreement, and changes were made, but I used their most widely accepted groupings.

Step 2 (Categorizing):

Equipment	Rules	Positions	Feelings
Bat	runs	catcher	losing
bases	fouls	pitcher	arguing
gloves	strikes	shortstop	fun
field	innings	fielder	winning
ball	outs		

Order of Importance

Next I asked the students to number the categories according to how interesting or important they were to the main topic, using one as the highest ranking. I also had them rank the words in the category chosen to be number one. I didn't require this for the other categories yet, so that this first assignment wouldn't be overwhelming.

Step 3 (Ranking)

#1	#2	#3	#4
Equipment	Rules	Positions	Feelings
bat #1			
bases #4			
gloves #5			
field#3			
ball #2			

When the categories were ranked, I transformed the first list—"Equipment"—into an oral paragraph. Then I asked for volunteers to compose paragraphs orally for each of the remaining categories. This oral practice gave the children hints on how to rank and organize each category's list of words.

To start the children off with writing, I did the first paragraph on the board. I explained that often, in nonfiction writing, the category's title is used in the topic sentence to introduce the paragraph. Then I used the words from the list in sentences to fill out the body of the paragraph.

Step 4 (Composing):

> *Baseball is one sport that doesn't require much equipment. You need only a bat, a ball and a field. You have to have bases, too, but they can be marks on the ground. A glove can keep the ball from hurting your hand, but you don't really need one.*

After leading the students through this approach a few more times, I encouraged them to choose topics of personal interest and develop them independently. I asked them to hand in the preparatory steps along with their compositions.

Later, as the students became more adept at paragraphing, I sometimes reversed steps 1 and 2: the students thought of the categories first and then sought to develop supporting details.

Learn from the Experts

Up to this point my approach to paragraphing had been inductive, but to reinforce the concept I asked the students to analyze paragraphs from publications. Through this deductive process, I hoped they could determine a professional writer's reason for the way he or she starts each paragraph.

I posted a chart of reasons for paragraph changes for my students to consult. It read: "We start a new paragraph for a different (1) time, (2) place/setting, (3) speaker, or (4) topic/point/

step/idea/event/etc." Then, from a book easily read by the majority of the students, I duplicated several paragraphs. With the posted list as a reference, the students determined as a group why the author began each paragraph and then each wrote the numbered reason (from the chart) in the paragraph's indentation. After we analyzed several paragraphs together, the students continued independently.

I varied this deductive approach by copying a passage from another easily read book—without showing the paragraph indentations. After reading the entire passage to the class, I asked where and why the second, third, and remaining paragraphs should begin. There was some disagreement, but I explained that no one way of paragraphing is *absolutely* correct and that different divisions are acceptable if the rationales are reasonable.

Then the students worked independently (sometimes in groups), rewriting other passages into paragraphs. They indicated the reason for each new paragraph in the indentation with a number from the chart.

A Necessary Skill

In a world filled with computer printouts and audiovisual gadgetry, composition writing is still a necessary communication skill. A great deal more can be taught about writing, especially in terms of quality. But it's difficult if children lack a basic understanding of organization or structure. To make writing simple, start with the paragraph.

Recommended Resources

Linden, Myra and Arthur Whimbey. *Why Johnny Can't Write: How to Improve Writing Skills.* Hillsdale, NJ: Lawrence Erlbaum Associates, 1990.

[Yes, it's 1990, but we still find Shakespeare useful, too. These are experienced teachers who reveal the shortcomings of "the 'process' (to writing) and its offspring, 'writing across the curriculum'." They laud the "sentence combining" procedure—proven successful and backed by research. Although a scholarly, in-depth look at what they consider the current, sorry practices of teaching writing, and their recommendations on how to rectify this, the book is a surprisingly easy and engrossing read. Suitable for teachers of grades four and up. It is available as new and used and top-rated by customers at Amazon.com.]

Frank, Marjorie. *If You're Trying to Teach Kids How to Write ... You've Gotta Have This Book!* Nashville: Incentive Publications, 1996.

[This is not an in-depth, philosophical treatment of writing (though some may say the author accomplishes it indirectly), but an example-after-example, fun activity tool for teachers—sprinkled with nuggets of wisdom throughout. For those who find such things useful this latest edition includes rubrics, portfolio assessment, and writing across the curriculum. Even if you find only a small portion helpful, the purchase is worth the price. Suitable for primary through middle school. This book is paperback and also available as new or used at Amazon.com where the customers top rate it.]

Chapter 2

"Memory Writing"

A Powerful Method for Teaching Paragraphing and Compositions—A Step-by-Step Approach

Students will welcome the idea that there is a non-onerous, concrete method that will help them get thoughts onto paper and then aid them in organizing those thoughts. Teachers—even more so—welcome such a technique. Herein, you will be led, step by step, to make students *understand* paragraphing, and from that, a whole composition.

There is a section for the simplest application of this idea (for primary grades) to more mature use (grades 4 or 5 through high school). More can be written about style, word choice, voice, audience, and other eventual necessities of writing, but without basic organizational skills, herein taught, what good are such accessories?

A Comparison

Memory writing is similar to diary and letter writing in that it can be personal, but there's a greater elapse of time—and, perhaps, it's easier. It is similar to autobiography except that only one incident in one's life is written about.

What the Student Learns

In "memory writing" students tap their memories and learn how to select and shape this material into compositions. They can use this memory-recalling process for later self-direction.

They will learn to work in small interacting-collaborating groups; deal with their egocentric, unelaborated writing; and pick up skill in sentence mechanics, grammar, and spelling.

They can be led to *sense* the need for paragraph divisions.

Why the Student Learns

The appeal of "memory writing" seems to be the personal content to which significant feelings are attached.

Nevertheless, this is not diary writing. Therefore, the students should be made aware of two kinds of writing: private and public. Diary writing is private (which, of course, can be made public later); memory writing (as a class activity) is public. But because it *is* personal disclosure, the students are urged not to write anything they would never want to reveal about themselves.

Another appeal (though maybe not at first if the students have never done this before) is the triad collaboration and editing as one is composing. This interaction is both socially and academically stimulating.

Finally, make the students aware beforehand—or sometime during the process—that they will be sharing their finalized products in a class booklet. This adds appeal to the task.

How the Student Learns: The Process

Lead the whole class together at first. Demonstrate memory writing by recalling your pleasant (or unpleasant) memories on the overhead projector or chalkboard as outlined below. After you have started or finished each step, stop and let the students do likewise.

Step 1 (Use this as a column-like title)

Search your memory for those childhood experiences/incidences of which you are fond (or otherwise): ones that will disclose something about you of which your students are unaware. (For the students it may be an incident that happened on a particular day, such as: first day in school, first bike, first fight, best trip, taking a music lesson, or old girl/boyfriend.)

If you feel better prepared by writing your memories down beforehand, then just copy them from your paper. Regardless, list them as brief notes for the students to see. Once you have written three or four they will get the idea. Ask them to join you. Let everyone spend ten minutes racking their brains. No talking.

Step 2 (And column two)

Choose one of your experiences listed during Step 1 and place it in the second column—one that you think would interest other people. (You can have this prepared beforehand, too.) Under this incident or memory list as many one-word or short-note details as you can that are connected with the memory. In other words, jot down everything you can remember about the incident, including your thoughts and feelings at the time. Allow fifteen minutes of class time for the students to do likewise.

Step 3 (Initial student sharing)

Students get into threesomes of their choice (or your appointment) and share their expanded memory (Step 2) by slowly (kids rattle things off much too fast) reading their memory title and the details. The other two members of the group rely upon their natural curiosity and ask any questions that strike them about the topic or what they think should be brought out by the writer. The composer can consider these possible elaborations. They can also state which of the details interest them most—helping the composer successfully prepare for his/her audience.

Step 4 (Writing those drafts)

Now comes the narrative composing. (Brace yourself for the groans and don't tell them this is only the *beginning* of the end.) Again, demonstrate (you may have prepared beforehand) how you're going to take those details listed in Step 2 and incorporate them into your story. For example, you may have numbered them chronologically or according to importance or interest. You may also have crossed some out for whatever reason: not closely enough related to the incident, too personal, or judged not interesting enough.

Step 5 (May take place next day)

After completion of writing their memory as a rough draft, the students have to prepare them not for you but for two other peers (their triad) to read and praise and criticize (helpfully).

These students will make written marginal suggestions or ask for clarification and deal with grammar and *mechancis* (such as that). Everybody in the group gets the same treatment.

Step 6 (Final draft)

The final draft must be accepted by the threesome. It will go into the class booklet without additional teacher modification (well

… if it's *really* unclear or you plan to share the booklet with other classes …).

Notes

Students keep their Step 1 memories for future memory writing. (Best to have a class file so the papers don't get lost.) Don't overdo this type of writing or procedure, but do play it for what it is worth.

The groans will start to disappear as the students start to enjoy and see the worth of collaborating with, sharing with, and learning from each other.

But let's be realistic here, too. If managing your class is difficult and student interaction tends to create bedlam, then skip the sharing part; it is not sacrosanct. Your students will still learn a great deal from this approach minus the social-interaction element.

HOW I DID IT

Step 1	*Step 2
going barefoot*	springtime/May 1st
building log cabins	sensitive feet-callused
picking berries & wild grapes	hot road
our swimming hole	cool grass
playing driving with sticks	ages 5–13/14
sister & washing	sundays
spoiled brother	mud
working on the farm	visiting
first girlfriend	nails, glass
picking in tomato field	leading the mule
one-room schoolhouse	bike riding
first-grade teacher	washing feet
	reason for stopping
	dreading new school year
	saved money—poor

Step 6

"Going Barefoot"

When I was between the <u>ages of 5 and 13</u> *I loved to go barefoot. One of the reasons my brothers, sisters, and I went without shoes after school and in the summer was because* <u>we were poor</u> *and could save our shoes some wear. But we would have wanted to go barefoot even if we were rich.*

We just couldn't wait until the <u>first day of May</u> *because that was when our foster mother let us first take off our shoes. We'd beg her before, especially if the weather was warm, but she'd not budge. I never knew why.*

On the first few days our feet were very <u>sensitive</u>. The dirt <u>road was very hot</u> to our feet and the smallest stone would bring an ouch and a jump. But after a couple weeks we could even run races on the road because the bottoms of our feet had a tough <u>callus</u> on them. The best place to walk was in the <u>grass of the lawn</u>. And it was fun to go to the creek and walk in the bed while <u>the mud</u> oozed up between our toes. It was so cool and refreshing!

Once, I stepped on a rusty <u>nail</u> and had to get a tetanus shot so I wouldn't get lockjaw. But in those days we did not have to fear broken glass because we lived in the country and children didn't break bottles like they did much later; they could take empties back to the store and get some money for them. We kids used to collect bottles to make a little spending money.

<u>Sundays</u> I hated, not because I had to go to church, but because after going barefoot all week (which made my feet a little bigger) shoes squeezed-up and hurt my feet something terrible (as country folk put it). This is one reason, too, I <u>dreaded going back to school</u> in September, because I would have to wear shoes all day. My feet would be burning with an awful pain at the end of each school day for a week or so. But eventually my feet got used to being imprisoned again.

I remember that we had a very large garden and used a mule (an animal that is part horse and part donkey) to help plow (dig up) the ground. It was usually my job to hold and <u>lead the mule</u> by his bridle (which was around his head and face) so he wouldn't step on the plants we were growing or bite off (eat) too many of them. Once in a while I would forget I was barefoot and walk too close to the mule's hoof (foot) and he would step right on my foot. Wow! Did that hurt. And the dumb mule didn't even know—and couldn't feel—he was on my foot. I'd push and shove at this heavy animal, but he'd move off very slowly—just considered my foot a clod of dirt, I guess. Then I'd have to sit down to rub and rub my sore foot. (Sometimes I'd put on some big old shoes for this job.)

I think everybody, even grownups, should go barefoot just to see how good it feels—even if it does hurt once in a while.

I purposely underlined the words or phrases I used in Step 2, above, because I wanted you to notice that I decided that every item from the list just didn't fit, so I didn't use them. But as I was writing I started remembering more, and I wrote it down.

Adaptations

For the early grades, a *Book about Me* dictated to an older child or aide for the student to illustrate is a good starting point. Pages can be, for example, "My Family," "My Toys," "When I Was a Baby."

For older students the taking of pictures of people, places, and things that are an important part of their life—parents, friends, house or bedroom, favorite possessions—and presenting them in an organized way with commentary can be a simple beginning or later version of "memory writing." (If doing this, rubber-cement the pictures to poster board and run through a continuous laminator found in teacher stores [least expensive method] or at larger photocopying/printing stores. Then tape the posters in the hallway for all to admire.)

Some "Memory Book" Titles

Down Memory Lane with 310	*Our Secret Crimes*
Trips into the Past	*Events from the Past*
History of a Friendship (or Enemy-ship)	*The Story of Our Lives*
I Absolutely, Positively Will Not Tell You About...(Secrets of 310)	*Yesteryear*
All About Me: Autobiographies	*Yakety-Yak: What 310 Has to Say*
Now You Know: Revelations of 310	*Revelations: Secret & Otherwise*
To Know Me is to Love Me	*Stop Laughing! (Our Embarrassing Moments)*
Say that Again? (Interviews with 310)	*Inside (Me) Edition*
This-'n'-That	

A Bonus? Rubric to Judge Compositional Writing

The Educational Powers That Be are currently on a binge, following the portfolio-rubric fad, so I offer the following clear, and hopefully acceptable, rubric (criteria for judging a piece of prose) that is easy for you and will get the above mentioned off your back.

Student meets some, all, or exceeds expectations for the current grade (or present skills taught) in the following areas:

1. Shows clarity of sentences and whole piece.

2. Meets objective of type of writing assigned: narrative, descriptive, persuasive, etc.

3. Sticks to the point (no extraneous ideas).

4. Reflects knowledge of mechanics: paragraphs (when to), punctuation, word agreement, spelling, capitalization, neatness.

5. Demonstrates depth: topic appropriately developed/ elaborated/explored as grade level of student might allow.

6. Related to numbers 1 and 3: exhibits organizational skills (logical order of ideas) in paragraphs and whole piece.

7. Optional: displays evident style—energy/emotions, humor, etc.

Chapter 3

Teaching Book Reports?

Do It Right

Yawn, yawn? The way to keep from putting your students to sleep is to give them an assignment that will not allow mundane thinking or copying. (I cringe when I pass a bulletin board full of neatly written reports and ninety-five percent are verbatim copying from the book or its flap.)

So, force your students to think, allow them to be creative, and don't worry about the number of books read—no matter what the District or a particular program desires. But do emphasize reading depth, which will vary for different grades or skill levels.

Additionally, there is a rule that I've always taught by: only direct your students to do a particular type of assignment when you have done an example assignment with them and given them a clear, physical facsimile of such a task. If you want them to do a historical fiction book report, read such a book to the class. Then, together, do a report on the book in the fashion you wish them to do later with another historical fiction book of their own choosing. This will lessen frustration, increase confidence, give you a better product to mark, and, hopefully, give the student a better letter grade.

The following examples are suitable for middle school through high school. Just reproduce appropriate pages and share with your students.

Fanciful Fiction Book Report

1. Fanciful stories have parts or ideas that couldn't really happen—are truly make-believe. What is fanciful about the story you read? (There may be more than one "fantastic" idea.)

2. Who are the bad guys in your story and why are they bad?

3. Just like any good story, there is a problem. What problem does the main character in your story have?

4. How does the main character get out of this problem?

5. Finally, you must write an ad for your book. Following are some examples to give you a feel for what I want. Tell something about the story plot (the way things happen), but leave the reader of your ad guessing about the story; you can do it: be slick.

Note: You must read your whole story. Then think, think, and think and try, try, try.

My Robot Buddy

By Alfred Slote

Can a robot be a friend? Jack thinks so—even if his father's not sure. Nevertheless Jack gets Danny for a birthday present. He's programmed to play sports, climb trees, and be happy. Be happy? Well ... he's a very expensive robot. (And that's why a robot snatcher is lurking nearby.)

Pippi Longstocking

By Astrid Lindgren

"Pippi Longstocking lived alone and had no mother and no father, and that was of course very nice because" … you know how grownups can get in the way of having fun. And fun is what Pippi had: some of it impossible, most of it unlikely, and the rest of it nonsense—that is, unless, you're Pippi. Level-headed Tommy and Annika couldn't resist Pippi's friendly but unusual ways, and you'll find it hard to do, too.

Charlotte's Web

By E. B. White

Can a spider save a pig from death—from becoming ham and bacon? Not ordinarily. But Charlotte is no ordinary spider, and Charlotte's Web is no ordinary story. There's young Fern, who can understand animal talk; and Templeton, who is a rat in more ways than one; poor Wilbur, a pig with an uncertain future; and, of course, Charlotte, our heroine—a very intelligent spider.

Biography Book Report # 1

Book: *Malcolm X* by Arnold Adoff

[This is a primary grade book; others about Malcom X are of varied difficulty.]

Outline

    I. Birth and Childhood
    II. Education/Training
    III. Accomplishments
    IV. Why S/he Can Be Admired

Written Report

Malcolm X is a book about a black man who became famous because he was not afraid to speak out against the way blacks were treated by whites.

Malcolm was born in 1925. His father was a minister who spoke up for black people's rights. Because of this the Klu Klux Klan tried to frighten him by burning down his house and doing other terrible things.

After Malcolm's father died (or was killed), his mother was put into a mental institution. Before long, Malcolm got into trouble and was put into a detention home run by whites who did not really like blacks. When Malcolm was released from there he had an eighth-grade education.

He lived in Boston afterward and went from bad to worse: selling dope and stolen liquor, and working for gangsters. When he was caught he was sent to prison.

In a way, being in prison helped prepare Malcolm for his future. He began to educate himself about black history, and became very knowledgeable about it. He also became a Black Muslim and a friend of Elijah Muhammed, the leader of that religion.

When Malcolm got out of prison he helped Elijah Muhammad speak for black pride and the rights of black people. He was such a good speaker he became loved by many blacks and disliked by many whites. (Although some blacks disliked him, too, because he eventually left the Black Muslims.) He became famous. But he was always threatened. And while about to make a speech one day, he was shot and killed.

I can admire Malcolm X because he studied hard and improved himself and was very brave to speak against white prejudice at a time when he could have been killed.

Speaking Notes

1. Introduction	5. Detention Home	9. Religion
2. Father	6. Boston	10. Speaking
3. KKK	7. Prison	11. Threats
4. Mother	8. Black History	12. Admire

Note: Start your first sentence as follows: "_____ is a book about...." (This is the main idea of your book). Start your last paragraph with, "I can admire _____ because...."

Biography Book Report # 2

Book: *Malcolm X* by Arnold Adoff

Questions

1. Why was the subject/person famous?

2. What were some problems the subject had to overcome to be successful? Write about one of these.

3. Tell how one person was important in helping the subject become famous—or reach his or her goal in life. (If there were no such important people, how did the subject overcome his or her problems alone to become famous?)

4. Describe the subject's appearance and personality. You may quote from the book.

5. Retell in your own words the most interesting happening in the story.

6. What did you admire most about the subject?

Possible Answers

1. Malcom X helped black people think of fighting for their rights. He taught blacks to be proud of themselves.

2. He had to overcome white racism and his own behavior in crime and drugs.

3. While Malcolm was in prison, Elijah Muhammad gave him hope (something to live for) by writing to him. He also helped Malcolm become famous by giving him an important position in his organization, the Nation of Islam.

4. Malcolm was very tall, handsome, and had freckles. Before he became religious, he was very mean in prison.

5. I thought two parts were very interesting. First is when Malcolm was in prison. He had nothing to do but read, and because of this he learned, for the first time, about the history of black people. This helped change his life. Also interesting, but also sad, was when he broke away from the Nation of Islam. He was hated by some whites and blacks, for different reasons, because of this. He was threatened a lot, and was soon shot to death.

6. I admire Malcolm X because he was willing to continue his work in spite of threats against his life.

Historical Fiction Book Report

Book: *Jump Ship to Freedom* by James Collier

[Junior high through high school level]

Questions

1. Give the book title and author.

2. Mention the main character and one other.

3. What strengths (positive character traits) does the main character possess?

4. Give an example of when one of the above strengths comes into play in the story.

5. Being human, the main character has weaknesses, too. Mention a weakness and tell how it affects the main character's life.

6. What values (worthy or admirable ideas) do you think the main character strongly believes in? How does s/he show one of these beliefs in the story?

7. What is the main character's hope(s)?

8. Fear(s)?

9. Your story takes place at a different time in history. Explain how life is different in those days or what is going on in that part of the country or world at the time.

10. Most good, serious stories end up teaching us something that will stay with us in our minds and hearts. What do you think the author would want us to remember after we've forgotten the details of this story?

11. Give a very general short description/review/synopsis of the story.

Possible Answers

1. The book is *Jump Ship to Freedom* by James Collier.

2. Arabus—a teenage slave who is determined to not let his master keep him and his mother slaves forever. Captain Ivers—a slave master who stole Arabus's and his mother's freedom money, and plans to sell him deeper into slavery in the West Indies.

3. Arabus is hardworking, eager to learn, shows determination, persistence, courage, and dedication to his mother.

4. Arabus's master stole his mom's "soldiers notes" that could be cashed-in later for money and used to buy Arabus's and his mother's freedom. Arabus stole them back. When suspected of this "thievery," he was beaten, but was determined not to confess.

5. Led to believe it due to his enslavement, Arabus thought of himself as intellectually inferior to whites. Thus, when he failed at something he sadly excused his failure with this reason. It took some convincing by others to help him try to overcome this attitude toward himself.

6. Arabus frequently dealt with the idea of fairness. The law seemed to say that anything a slave "owns" really belongs to the master because the master owns the slave. Arabus's father took his master's place and fought in the Revolutionary War. Thus, Arabus's father earned his freedom and soldiers notes (a legal promise to pay), which may later be tuned into real

money. Arabus's mother is forced to turn over the notes to Captain Ivers's wife when Arabus's father dies. It is said to be for "safe keeping," but all know they will not be returned. This seems unfair to Arabus and his mother, who steal the notes back. And the rest of the story grows from this idea.

7. Arabus's hope is to buy his and his mother's freedom using the notes of his dead father.

8. Arabus's continual fear is that he may lose his father's soldier's notes, be caught, and sold off to the West Indies—never to see his mother again.

9. The setting of this story is post-Revolutionary War times. Colonial leaders are attending the Constitutional Convention in Philadelphia and anti-slavery individuals—Quakers, mostly—are trying to persuade the colonial representatives to deal with the subject of slavery in the constitution.

10. The author probably wants us to learn of the treatment of slaves and a little about the Constitutional Convention in Philadelphia.

11. *Jump Ship to Freedom* is a suspenseful story of the narrow escapes and determined efforts of a runaway slave.

THE BOOK INTERVIEW

For this assignment you will have to be very knowledgeable about the book you have read. You will be interviewed about the book in front of the class similarly to how it is done on a TV or radio talk show.

You will be expected to know the answer to the following questions, but other follow-up questions may also be asked. You will be evaluated on your performance in two areas: speaking ability and knowledge of your book. If you know the answers to the questions below you will have a good start. If, for some reason, you are not able to give an answer to a question, then you should offer a good reason. Try not to go on and on about the book in answer to a question, but do answer thoroughly and elaborate when you think it is helpful to your audience's understanding or enjoyment. Bring your book to the interview.

Your interviewer may be the teacher, an aide, a qualified student, any combination of these, or a panel.

The questions have been listed under categories. You should be familiar with the category terms because these may be used in a question, and they will be used in high school in literature study.

Questions

Setting (The physical scene and initial and other situation/s)

1. Tell about the place(s) where the story happens.

Plot (The story's plan, unfolding)

2. What does the main character want and why?

3. What helps him/her reach this goal?

4. What are some events that hinder him/her?

5. Besides the climax (see below), what was an exciting event in the story?

Climax (The final important event)

> 6. What finally helps the main character get what s/he has been seeking?

> 7. If the main character doesn't reach his/her goal, why—or what does happen?

Mood (Feelings created by the story)

> 8. At certain times you had strong feelings when reading the book: suspense, anger, love, sympathy, and so on. Identify one of your feelings and tell about the event that created that mood.

Characterization (The personality given to a character)

> 9. Describe the main character's appearance and personality. You may quote from the book.

Theme/Moral (A statement the author is making through storytelling)

> 10. Does the story teach us any lesson or truth about behavior or beliefs? (This would be the same lesson one or more of the characters learned—even though the story may not mention that this lesson is learned.)

Realistic Fiction Book Report

(Write answers in full sentences and/or paragraphs.)

1. What book did you read? (Include title and author.)

2. Who are the most important characters? Describe them as follows:

   Jim: A slave who flees rather than be sold.

   Pap: Huck's drunken and mean father.

3. Where—in what place or kind of place—does the story happen?

4. Who is the main person—the hero or heroine—in the story?

5. What is the main problem or conflict in the story?

6. How is this problem solved?

7. How does the main character change? (How is s/he different at the end?)

8. What causes the main character to change?

9. What is the most important event and what makes it so?

10. Why do you think the author wrote this book?

11. Why would, or wouldn't, you recommend this book?

Handicapped Book Report

1. How differently did some react to this person's handicap?

2. What type of help did this person receive?

3. How did this person initially view his or her own "problem"?

4. How did this person deal with this handicap or challenge?

5. Most of us have had some brief or longer contact with a physically or mentally handicapped or emotionally disturbed person. Most people have such a close or distant relative. How do you emotionally react to (or feel toward) such a person? Maybe you react differently to different handicaps. Be honest.

6. Would you refuse to be a close friend to or date a person who is physically handicapped? Does it depend on the disability? Give your reason. (I don't have to agree with you for your answer to be right for you.)

Note: Head your paper with the book title and author.

Animal Story Book Report

1. What hardship (dangers or trials) did the animal experience?

2. Why?

3. What pleasure(s) did the animal experience?

4. What was the good or bad relationship like between the animal and an important human character?

5. What did you learn about this type of animal you did not know before?

6. Write a paragraph or more sharing your feelings about an animal you know or have known: a loving pet, attacking dog, how you reacted to someone else's treatment of an animal, and such.

Minority-Group Book Report

Questions

1. What was one thing (or more) you learned about this group you never knew before?

2. How are they different from you? (Language, customs, etc.)

3. How are they similar to you?

4. What special problems does this group have?

5. What special advantages does this group have? (Political, economic, cultural.)

6. Before reading the book, what feelings/knowledge did you have about this group? To what extent was this changed by reading the book?

7. If this was a fiction book, would you explain or retell the happiest/saddest/most comical event in the story?

8. If a fiction story, did you notice a change in the main character by the end of the story? How did s/he change? What caused this?

9. How do TV or the movies usually depict this group? (What seems to be accurate? Inaccurate?)

10. If fiction, which character did you like/dislike the most and why? (You can answer this for some non-fiction books, too.)

11. What lesson did any of the characters learn?

12. Did the story teach you any "truth" (lesson) about life?

13. What mostly made the book interesting to you?

Groups

"Subcultural" as used here means a minority group that practices distinctive activities traditionally associated with that group. Not all members of such groups set themselves apart by dress, association, or actions—and some are members of more than one group by marriage. Both fiction (novels) and informational books are written about such groups; if you need help, ask the librarian. (If you are a member of such a group, you are expected to read about another group.) The following list is far from exhaustive:

- Native Americans (Indians) or individual tribes
- Gypsies
- Rural people of Appalachia
- Ethnic or racial groups (Americans from, or with ancestors from, Poland, Russia, Ireland, Italy, Latin America, Asia, Africa, and many more)
- Religious groups (Amish, Mormons, Hasidic Jews, Black Muslims, etc.)

Other-Country Book Report

1. Book, title, author, copyright date?

Human and Physical Geography

2. Where do most people live and why? (Population distribution.)

3. How have the country's global (latitude and elevation) location, terrain, and (presently developed) natural resources affected the type and amount of the country's produce and industries?

Culture

4. What is a typical daily or weekly schedule for a (rural, village, or city) family?

5. What are the normal chronological highlights in a boy's or girl's life up to adulthood?

6. Discuss one or more minority groups. Are any discriminated against? If so, why and how?

7. List four customs (practices, group behaviors) that are unusual or different from customs in our country. Discuss a custom you like and one you didn't.

8. How is schooling different?

9. What might be a distinct family responsibility a boy or girl might have that would be different from your family?

10. Any unusual holidays or celebrations—not mentioned in number 7, above?

History

11. Was the country ever a colony—or did it *have* colonies? If either, discuss.

12. If the country was ever a colony, how did this affect the country's traditions for the worse or better?

13. Was there ever a period of slavery, slave trading/selling? If so, discuss.

14. Is there a most-famous person? Why is s/he famous?

Economics

15. Related to question 3, what makes the country's valuable crops and industries valuable?

16. Percentage-wise, where/how is the average family income spent?

International Relations

17. How important are the country's neighbors, economically and culturally?

18. What economic, cultural, religious relationships does the country have with us? (Examples: Peace Corps, missionaries, movies, TV programs, financial aid.)

19. What is the predominate view(s) expressed about the U.S.?

THUMBS UP, THUMBS DOWN

STUDENT-RATED BOOKS

BOOK TITLE	1	2	3	4	5	STUDENT RATER

RATINGS: (1) Too uninteresting to finish; (2) Finished, but it isn't that great; (3) It is okay; (4) Better than most—at least *I* like it; (5) So good anyone would like it..

To the teacher: enlarge as needed. Could scan and make title red, subtitle blue, etc.

Historical Fiction Book List

Organized alphabetically by author. Topic and suggested reading/interest level for some (in parentheses). Most are intermediate through junior high.

Aaron, Chester
GIDEON
(Holocaust)

Annixter, Jane
BUFFALO CHIEF
(Indian)

Armstrong, William H.
SOUNDER
(Prejudice) (I)

Baker, Betty
AND ONE WAS A WOODEN INDIAN
(Indian)
STRANGER AND AFRAID
(Spanish Explorers) (I)

Beatty, John
WHO COMES TO KING MOUNTAIN?
(revolutionary WAr) (JH)

Beatty, Patricia
TURN HOMEWARD, HANNALEE
(Civil War)
WAIT FOR ME, WATCH FOR ME, EULA BEE
(Civil War)

Benchley, Nathaniel
GONE AND BACK
(Indian)
ONLY EARTH AND SKY LASTS FOREVER
(Indian)

Bolton, Carole
NEVER JAM TODAY
(Women's right to vote)

Bonham, Frank
CHIEF
(Indian)

Bruckner, Karl
THE DAY OF THE BOMB
(World War II / Japan)

Burchard, Peter
BIMBY
(Civil War) (I)

Carlson, Natalie S.
EMPTY SCHOOL HOUSE, THE
(Prejudice) (I)

Cavana, Betty
RUFFLES AND DRUMS
(Rev. War) (I-JH)
TOUCH OF MAGIC, A
(Rev. War)

Cheney, Cora
INCREDIBLE DEBORAH, THE
(Rev. War)

Clapp, Patricia
STORY OF EARLY PLY-MOUTH
(Colonial) (JH)

Clark, Ann Nolan
CIRCLE OF SEASONS
(Indian)

Clifford, Eth
YEAR OF THE THREE-LEGGED DEER
(Prejudice, Indian, Afro-Am.) (I-JH)

Climo, Shirley
MONTH OF SEVEN DAYS, A
(Civil War)

Collier, James
BLOODY COUNTRY, THE
(Rev. War) (I-JH)
JUMP SHIP TO FREEDOM
(Slavery, Colonial) (I-JH)
MY BROTHER SAM IS DEAD
(Rev. War) (I-JH)

Constant, Alberta
MISS CHARITY COME TO STAY
(Homesteading) (JH)

Corriveau, Monique
WAPITI, THE
(Indian, colonial)

Cummings, Betty S.
HEW AGAINST THE GRAIN
(Civil War) (JH)

Dank, Milton
DANGEROUS GAME, THE
(World War II, Nazis)

Davis, Daniel S.
BEHIND THE BARBED WIRE
(World War II, Japan-American) (JH)

De Jong, Meindert
HOUSE OF SIXTY FATHERS
(China)

Edwards, Sally
WHEN THE WORLD'S ON FIRE
(Rev. War) (JH)

Erlich, Amy
WOUNDED KNEE
(Indian) (JH)

Fast, Howard
FREEDOM ROAD
(Post-slavery)

Finlayson, Ann
GREENHORN ON THE FRONTIERS
(Pre-Rev. War, Pennsylvania) (I-JH)
REBECCA'S WAR

Fisher, Leonard E.
WARLOCK OF WEST-FALL
(Colonial, witches) (I-JH)

Fleischman, Sid
BY THE GREAT HORN SPOON

Flory, Jane
GOLDEN VENTURE
(Gold Rush)

Forbes, Esther
JOHNNY TREMAIN
(Rev. WAr)

Haynes, Betsy
COWSLIP
(Slavery) (I-JH)

Fox, Paula
SLAVE DANCER
(slavery) (JH)

Fritz, Jean
BRADY
(Slavery, underground RR) (I)
*CAN'T YOU MAKE THEM
BEHAVE, KING GEORGE?*
(Colonial) (P)
EARLY THUNDER
(Rev. War) (JH)

Garfield, Leon
SOUND OF COACHES, THE
(England)

Gessner, Lynne
NAVAJO SLAVE
(Indian Slavery)

Glasser, Dianne
DIARY OF TRILBY FROST
(Early 1900s)

Goble, Paul
*DEATH OF THE IRON
HORSE*
(Indian)

Graham, gAIL
*CROSS-FIRE: A VIETNAM
NOVEL*
(Vietnam War)

Hamilton, Virginia
HOUSE OF DIES DREAR
(Slavery)

Hansen, Joyce
WHICH WAY FREDOM
(Civil War, slavery)

Harris, Christie
RAVEN'S CRY
(Indian) (I)

Haugaard, Erik
*CHASE ME, CATCH
NOBODY!*
(Holocaust)
CROMWELL'S BOY
(Rev. War)
LEIF THE UNLUCKY
(Norsemen) (P)
SAMURAI'S TALE

Keneally, Thomas
SCHINDLER'S LIST
(World War II Holocaust)

Hickman, Janet
ZOAR BLUE
(Civil War)

Holm, Anne
NORTH TO FREEDOM
(Nazis) (I-JH)

Holman, Felice
WILD CHILDREN, THE
(Russia)

Hudson, Jan
SWEETGRASS
(Indian)

Hunt, Irene
ACROSS FIVE APRILS
(Civil War)
*NO PROMISES IN THE
WIND*
(Great Depression)

Irwin, Hadley
I BE SOMEBODY
(Slavery)

Johnston, Norma
KEEPING DAYS, THE

Jones, Douglas C.
CREEK CALLED WOUNDED KNEE, A
(Indian)

Jones, Peter
REBEL IN THE NIGHT
(Rev. War)

Josephs, Anna C.
MOUNTAIN BOY
(Civil War)

Keith, Harold
RIFLES FOR WATIE
(Civil War) (I-JH)

Kelly, Eric P.
TRUMPETER OF KRAKOW

Meltzer, Milton
UNDERGROUND MAN: A NOVEL
(Abolitionists) (I-JH)

Kerr, Judith
WHEN HITLER STOLE PINK RABBIT
(World War II, Holocaust) (I)

Kraske, Robert
SEA ROBBERS
(Colonial pirates) (JH)

Laurintzen, Jonreed
ORDEAL OF THE YOUNG HUNTER
(Indian) (I)

Lester, julius
THIS STRANGE NEW FEELING
(Post-Civil War)

Levitin, Sonia
JOURNEY TO AMERICA
(Holocaust) (I)
ROANOKE:NOVEL OF THE LOST COLONY
(Colonial) (JH)

Lobdell, Helen
FORT IN THE FOREST
(Colonial: French-Indian War) (JH)

Lord, Athena
SPIRIT TO RIDE THE WHIRLWIND
(Colonial)

Lowry, Lois
NUMBER THE STARS
(World War II, Holocaust) (I-JH)

Maeri, Louise
SAVE THE QUEEN OF SHEBA

Magorian, Michelle
GOOD NIGHT, MR. TOM
(World War II)

McHargue, Georgess
MEET THE WITCHES
(Colonial)

Meader, Stephen
WHO RIDES IN THE DARK
(Rev. War)
FRIEDRICH
(Holocaust)
I WAS THERE
(Hitler's Germany)

Monjo, F. N.
SLATER'S MILL
(Colonial)

Morpurgo, Michael
WAITING FOR ANYA
(World War II, Holocaust) (JH)

Moskin, Marietta D.
I AM ROSEMARIE
(Holocaust)

O'Dell, Scott
ISLAND OF THE BLUE DOL-PHIN
(Indian) (I-JH)
KING'S FIFTH, THE
(Explorers)
SING DOWN THE MOON
(Indian) (I-JH)
THUNDER ROLLING IN THE MOUNTAIN
(Indian)

Orlev, Uri
ISLAND ON BIRD STREET, THE
(Holocaust)

Paterson, Katherine
MASTER PUPPETEER, THE
(18th-century Japan)
SIGN OF THE CHRYSAN-THEMUM
(Medieval Japan)

Peck, Robert N.
RABBITS AND RED-COATS
(Rev. War) (I)

Perez, N. A.
ONE SPECIAL YEAR
(Smalltown, USA)

Petry, Ann
TITUBA OF SALEM VIL-LAGE
(Colonial, witches) (JH)

Phelan, Mary Kay
FOUR DAYS IN PHILA-DELPHIA—1776
(Rev. War)
MIDNIGHT ALARM: THE STORY OF PAUL REVERE'S RIDE
(Rev. War)

Richter, Conrad
LIGHT IN THE FOREST
(Indian) (JH)

Rockwood, Joyce
LONG MAN'S SONG
(Indian) (JH)
TO SPOIL THE SUN
(Indian) (JH)

Sachs, Marilyn
CALL ME RUTH
(Jewish immigrants)

Sorensen, Virginia
PLAIN GIRL
(Amish)

Smucker, Barbara
**RUNAWAY TO FREEDOM:
A STORY OF THE UNDER-
GROUND RAILWAY**
(Slavery)

Sneve, Virginia
BETRAYED
(Civil War: Indian-white conflicts) (I)

Speare, Elizabeth
CALICO CAPTIVE
(Indian)
SIGN OF THE BEAVER
(Colonial)
**WITCH OF BLACKBIRD
POND**
(Colonial, witches) (I-JH)

Steele, William
PERLOUS ROAD
(Civil War) (I)

Sterling, Dorothy
MARY JANE

Stuart, Morna
**MARASSA AND MID-
NIGHT**
(Slavery)

Sutcliff, Rosemary
OUTCAST
(England)

Symons, Geraldine
**MISS RIVERS AND MISS
BRIDGES**
(England, Women's rights)

Talbot, Charlene J.
**SODBUSTER VENTURE,
THE**
(Post-Civil War)

Taylor, Mildred
**ROLL OF THUNDER,
HEAR MY CRY**
(Prejudice, The Great Depres-
sion) (I-JH)
SONG OF THE TREES
(Prejudice, The Great Depres-
sion) (I-JH)

Taylor, Theodore
CAY, THE
(JH)
CHILDREN'S WAY
(World War II)

Thrasher, Crystal
END OF A DARK ROAD
(The Great Depression)

Travers, P. L.
I GO BY SEA
(World War II)

Treece, Henry
VIKINGS DAWN
(The Vikings)

Tunia, John
SILENCE OVER DUNKER-QUE
(World War II, Nazi) (JH)

Uchida, Yoshiko
BEST BAD THING, THE
(Japanese-Americans)

Underwood, Betty
TAMARACK TREE
(Prejudice) (JH)

Vining, Elizabeth G.
TAKEN GIRL, THE
(Colonial) (I-JH)

Wakasuki, Jeanne
FAREWELL TO MANZANAR
(World War II, Japanese-American) (JH)

Wallin, Luke
IN THE SHADOW OF THE WIND
(Prejudice)

Wartski, Maureen C.
BOAT TO NOWHERE, A
(Vietnamese "boat people")
LONG WAY FROM HOME, A
(Vietnamese War refugees

Weinman, Eiveen
WHICH WAY COURAGE
(Amish) (JH)

Wesler, Clifton G.
WINTER OF THE WOLF
(Civil War)

Wibberly, Leonard
JOHN TREEGATE'S MUS-KET
(Rev. War) (JH)
LAST BATTLE
(War of 1812) (JH)

Wojciechowska, Maia
SHADOW OF A BULL

Yep, Laurence
MOUNTAIN LIGHT
(Chinese)

Although more history than fiction, if permitted by your teacher, look into the *American Girl Series'* **WELCOME TO...** These intermediate-grade-reading-level books are definitely not just for girls; the stories are simply told with female main characters.

Consult your teacher, school, or public librarians for other recommended titles.

Animal Stories Book List

Organized alphabetically by author. Suggested reading/interest level for some (in parentheses). Most are intermediate through junior high.

Annixter, Jane
GREAT WHITE

Annixter, Paul
SWIFTWATER

Arnosky, Jim
GRAY BOY (I)

Bagnold, Enid
NATIONAL VELVET I-JH)

Baird, Leslie
TIC-TAC

Ball, Zachary
BRISTLE FACE

Bontemps, Arna
FAST SOONER HOUND

Burnford, Sheila
INCREDIBLE JOURNEY (I-JH)

Byars, Betsy
MIDNIGHT FOX (I-JH)

Carlson, Natalie
CHALOU

Gipson, Fred
OLD YELLER (I-JH)

Clark, Ann
BLUE CANYON HORSE

Cleary, Beverly
MISHMASH (I)
RIBSY (I)

Coatsworth, Elizabeth
JACK'S ISLAND

De Jong, Meindert
ALONG CAME A DOG
HURRY HOME, CANDY

Eckert, Allen
INCIDENT AT HAWK'S HILL (I-JH)

Ellis, Ella
ROAM THE WILD COUNTRY

Farley, Walter
BLACK STALLION (I)

Garfield, James
FOLLOW MY LEADER (I)

George, Jean Craighead
CRY OF THE CROW (I)
JULIE OF THE WOLVES (I-JH)

Gipson, Fred
OLD YELLER (I-JH)

Griffiths, Helen
GREYHOUND, THE

Henry, Marguerite
BRIGHTY OF THE GRAND CANYON (I)
KING OF THE WIND (I-JH)
JUSTIN MORGAN HAD A HORSE (I)
MISTY OF CHINCOTE-AGUE (I)

Hightower, Florence
DARK HORSE OF WOOD-FIELD

Kjelgaard, Jim
BIG RED (I)
DESERT DOG (I)
SNOW DOG (I-JH)
WILD TREK (I)

Knight, Eric
LASSIE COME-HOME (I-JH)

London, Jack
CALL OF THE WILD (I-JH)
WHITE FANG (I-JH)

Lippincott, Joseph
RED ROAN PONY

Merrill, Jean
SUPERLATIVE HORSE

MacKellar, William
DOG LIKE NO OTHER, A

McMeekin, Isabella
KENTUCKY DERBY WIN-NER

Morey, Walter
ANGRY WATERS (I-JH)
CANYON WINTER (I-JH)
GENTLE BEN (I-JH)
GLOOMY GUS (I-JH)
RUNAWAY STALLION (I-JH)

North, Sterling
RASCAL (I-JH)

O'Brien, Jack
SILVER CHIEF TO THE RESCUE

O'Hara, Mary
MY FRIEND FLICKA (I-JH)

Ottley, Reginald
ROAN COLT

Perrin, Blanche
HUNDRED HORSE FARM

Peyton, K. M.
FLY-BY-NIGHT

Rawlings, Marjorie
YEARLING, THE (I-JH)

Rawls, Wilson
SUMMER OF THE MON-KEYS (I)
WHERE THE RED FERN GROWS (I-JH)

Rounds, Glen
BLIND COLT (I)

Self, Margaret
SKY ROCKET

Sewell, Anna
BLACK BEAUTY (I-JH)

Smith, Vian
COME DOWN THE MOUN-TAIN

Street, James
GOODBYE MY LADY

Tolan, Stephanie S.
TIME TO BE FREE

Viereck, Phillip
SUE'S SECONDHAND HORSE

Walker, David
BIG BEN

Will, James
SMOKEY, THE COW-HORSE (I-JH)

Wojiechowska, Maia
KINGDOM IN A HORSE

Consult your teacher, school or public librarians for other recommended titles.

Handicapped Book List

Organized alphabetically by author. Suggested reading/interest level for some (in parenthesis). Intermediate through junior high grades.

Albert, Louise
BUT I'M READY TO GO (JH)

Armer, Alberta
SCREWBALL (I)

Babbis, Friis
DON'T TAKE TEDDY (I-JH)

Baker, Louise
OUT ON A LIMB (JH)

Brown, Fern G.
YOU'RE SOMEBODY SPE-CIAL ON A HORSE (JH+)

Clifton, Lucile
MY FRIEND JACOB

Corcoran, Barbara
AXE-TIME, SWORD-TIME (JH)
DANCE TO STILL MUSIC, A (JH)

Ellis, Ella Thorp
CELEBRATE THE MORN-ING (I-JH)

Garfield, James
FOLLOW MY LEADER (I)

Blume, Judy
DEENIE

Brown, Roy
ESCAPE THE RIVER (JH)

Butler, Beverly
GIFT OF GOLD (JH+)
LIGHT A SINGLE CANDLE (JH+)

Byers, Betsy
SUMMER OF THE SWANS (I)

Chvigny, Hector
MY EYES HAVE A COLD NOSE (JH)

Kent, Deborah
ONE STEP AT A TIME

Killilea, Maria
KAREN (JH)
WREN

Klein, Gerda
BLUE ROSE, THE (JH)

Konigsburg, E. L.
GEORGE (JH)

Greenburg, Joanne
I NEVER PROMISED YOU A ROSE GARDEN (JH)

Gunther, John
DEATH BE NOT PROUD

Harr, Jaap Ter
WORLD OF BEN LIGHT-HART, THE (JH)

Heide, Florence
GROWING ANYWAY UP (I)

Hunter, Edith F.
CHILD OF THE SILENT NIGHT (JH+)

Hunter, Mollie
STRONGHOLE, THE (JH)

Johnson, Emily R.
SPRING AND SHADOW MAN (I-JH)

Keller, Helen
STORY OF MY LIFE (JH)

Pollock, Penny
KEEPING IT SECRET (I)

Putnam, Peter
KEEP YOUR HEAD UP, MR. PUTNAM (JH)

Platt, Kin
BOY WHO COULD MAKE HIMSELF DISAPPEAR, THE (JH+)

Lee, Mildred
SKATING RINK, THE

Little, Jean
MINE FOR KEEPS (I)
TAKE WING (I)

Lund, Doris
ERIC

Marshall, Alan
I CAN JUMP PUDDLES (JH)

Martin, Ann N.
WITH YOU AND WITH-OUT YOU (I-JH)

Mehta, Vid
FACE TO FACE (JH)

Melton, David
BOY CALLED HOPELESS, A

Neufield, John
LISA, BRIGHT AND DARK (JH+)

Shyer, Marlene F.
WELCOME HOME, JELLY-BEAN (I)

Slepian, Jan
ALFRED SUMMER, THE (JH)

Slote, Alfred
HANG TOUGH, PAUL MATHER (I)

Reynolds, Pamela
*DIFFERENT KIND OF SIS-
TER (I)*

Rinaldo, C. L.
DARK DREAMS

Robinson, Veronica
DAVID IN SILENCE (I)

Rodowsky, Colby
WHAT ABOUT ME? (JH)

Savitz, Harriet
*FLY, WHEELS, FLY (I-JH)
LIONHEARTED, THE (I-JH)
ON THE MOVE (I-JH)*

Smith, Doris
KELLY'S CREEK (I-JH+)

Southhall, Ivan
LET THE BALLOON GO

Spence, Eleanor
DEVIL HOLE, THE (JH)

Wartski, Maureen C.
*MY BROTHER IS SPECIAL
(JH)*

Yates, Elizabeth
*SKEEZER, A DOG WITH A
MISSION (I-JH)*

Consult your teacher, school, or public librarian for other recommended titles.

Fantasy/Science Fiction Book List ·

Organized alphabetically by author. Suggested reading/interest level for some (in parentheses). Most are intermediate through junior high, but also some primary and high school for varied readers.

Alexander, Lloyd
THE BOOK OF THREE (I-JH)

Atwater, Richard & Florence
MR. POPPER'S PENGUINS (I-JH)

Babbitt, Natalie
THE EYES OF THE AMARYLLIS (JH-HS)

Bonham, Frank
THE MISSING PERSONS LEAGUE (I-JH)

Bova, Ben
EXILED FROM EARTH (I-JH)

Butterworth, William
NEXT STOP, EARTH (P-I)

Cameron, Eleanor
THE WONDERFUL FLIGHT TO THE MUSHROOM PLANET (I)

Chase, Richard
THE JACK TALES (I-HS)

Christopher, John
THE GUARDIANS (I-HS)
THE WHITE MOUNTAINS
WILD JACK (I-HS)

Cleary, Beverly
THE MOUSE AND THE MOTORCYCLE (I)

Dahl, Roald
JAMES AND THE GIANT PEACH (P-I)

Gag, Wanda
TALES FROM GRIMM (P-I)

Hieatt, Constance
THE KNIGHT OF THE LION (I)

Hoover, H.M.
THIS TIME OF DARKNESS (I-HS)

Hunter, Mollie
A STRANGER CAME ASHORE (I/JH-HS)

Kipling Rudyard
JUST SO STORIES (I-JH)

Lester, Julius
BLACK FOLK TALES (I/JH-HS)

L'Engle, Madeleine
A WRINKLE IN TIME (I-HS)

Lewis, C.S.
THE LION, THE WITCH, AND THE WARDROBE (I-JH/HS)

Lindgren, Astrid
PIPPI LONGSTOCKING (I)

McCaffrey, Anne
DRAGONSONG (I/JH-HS)

Norton, Andre
OUTSIDE (I-JH/HS)

Norton, Mary
THE BORROWERS (I-JH)

O'Brien, Robert C.
MRS. FRISBY AND THE RATS OF NIMH (I-JH)

Opie, Iona and Peter
THE CLASSIC FAIRY TALES (I-HS)

Panshin, Alexei
RITE OF PASSAGE (I-JH/HS)

Phelps, Ethel
TATTERHOOD AND OTHER TALES (I-JH)

Robertson, Dorothy
FAIRY TALES FROM VIETNAM (P-I)

Selden, George
THE CRICKET IN TIMES SQUARE (I-JH)

Sleator, William
HOUSE OF STAIRS (JH)

Slote, Alfred
MY ROBOT BUDDY (P-I)
MY TRIP TO ALPHA I(I)

Tolkien, J.R.R.
THE HOBBIT (I-JH/HS)

Townsend, John R.
NOAH'S CASTLE (I-HS)

White, E.B.
CHARLOTE'S WEB (I-JH)

Consult your teacher, school or public librarian for other recommended books.

Realistic Fiction Book List

Organized alphabetically by author. Suggested reading/interest level for some (in parentheses). Most are intermediate through junior high, but also some primary and high school for varied readers.

Anonymous
GO ASK ALICE (I-HS)

Adler, C.S.
IN OUR HOUSE SCOTT IS MY BROTHER (I-JH)

Blume, Judy
ARE YOU THERE, GOD? IT'S ME, MARGARET (I-JH) FRECKLE JUICE (P-I) TALES OF A FOURTH GRADE NOTHING (I-JH) THEN AGAIN, MAYBE I WON'T (I-JH/HS)

Bonham, Frank
COOL CAT (I-HS) DURANGO STREET (I-JH)

Branscum, Robbie
JOHNNY MAY (I-JH)

Bulla, Clyde Robert
EAGLE FEATHER (P-I)

Byars, Betsy C.
THE HOUSE OF WINGS (I-JH/HS) THE PINBALLS (I-JH/HS)

Childress, Alice
A HERO AIN'T NOTHIN' BUT A SANDWICH (I-HS)

Cleaver, Vera and Bill
I WOULD RATHER BE A TURNIP (I-JH/HS) WHERE THE LILIES BLOOM (I-JH/.HS)

Clymer, Eleanor
MY BROTHER STEVIE (I-JH)

Cormier, Robert
THE CHOCOLATE WAR (JH-HS) I AM THE CHEESE (JH-HS)

Crawford Charles P.
THREE-LEGGED RACE (I-JH/HS)

Danziger, Paula
CAN YOU SUE YOUR PAR-
ENTS FOR MALPRACTICE?
(I-JH/HS)
THE CAT ATE MY GYM-
SUIT (I-JH/HS)

Donovan, John
I'LL GET THERE: IT BET-
TER BE WORTH THE TRIP
(I-JH)

Duncan, Lois
KILLING MR. GRIFFIN (JH-
HS)

Estes, Eleanor
THE HUNDRED DRESSES
(P/I-JH)

Ewing, Kathryn
A PRIVATE MATTER (I)

Fitzgerald, John D.
THE GREAT BRAIN
REFORMS (I-JH)

Golding, William
LORD OF THE FLIES (JH-
HS)

Graham, Lorenz
SOUTH TOWN (I-HS)

Greene, Betty
PHILIP HALL LIKES ME: I
RECKON MAYBE (I-JH)

Greene, Constance C.
THE UNMAKING OF RAB-
BIT (I-JH/HS)

Hanlon, Emily
IT'S TOO LATE FOR
SORRY (I-JH)

Hentoff, Nat
JAZZ COUNTRY (I-JH)

Hinton, S.E.
RUMBLE FISH (I-HS)
THAT WAS THEN, THIS IS
NOW (I-HS)

Hunt, Irene
UP A ROAD SLOWLY (I-
JH)

Kerr, M.E.
IF I LOVE YOU, AM I
TRAPPED FOREVER? (I-
JH)
I'LL LOVE YOU WHEN
YOU'RE MORE LIKE ME
(I-JH)

Lexau, Joan M.
STRIPED ICE CREAM (I)

Lipsyte, Robert
THE CONTENDER (I-JH)

Lowry, Lois
A SUMMER TO DIE (I-JH/ HS)

Maddock, Reginald
THIN ICE (I-JH/HS)

Mann, Peggy
MY DAD LIVES IN A DOWNTOWN HOTEL (P-I)

Mazer, Harry
GUY LENNY (I-JH/HS)

Mazer, Norma
A FIGURE OF SPEECH (I-JH/HS)

Miles, Miska
GERTRUDE'S POCKET (P-I) HOAGIE'S RIFLE-GUN (P-I) MAUDIE AND ME AND THE DIRTY BOOK (P/I-JH)

Morganroth, Barbara
WILL THE REAL RENIE LAKE PLEASE STAND UP (I-JH/HS)

Newfield, Marcia
A BOOK FOR JODAN (P-I)

Paterson, Katherine
THE GREAT GILLY HOPKINS (I-JH/HS)

Peck, Richard
DON'T LOOK AND IT WON'T HURT (I-JH)

Perl, Lila
DUMB LIKE ME, OLIVIA POTTS (I-JH)

Rockwell, Thomas
HOW TO EAT FRIED WORMS (I-JH)

Sherburne, Zoa
TOO BAD ABOUT THE HAINES GIRL (I-JH/HS)

Sorensen, Virginia
PLAIN GIRL (I-JH)

Talbot, Charlene
CHILDREN IN HIDING (I-JH)

Wagner, Jane
J.T. (P-I)

Wojciechowska, Maia
TUNED OUT (I-JH)

Pascal, Francine
THE HAND ME DOWN KID (I-JH/HS)

Zindel, Paul
CONFESSIONS OF A TEENAGE BABOON (I-JH/HS)
MY DARLING, MY HAMBURGER (I-JH)
THE PIGMAN (JH-HS)

Chapter 4

Letter Writing

Don't Let It Become a Lost Art

Dear Teacher:

Are your students letter writers? (Most curriculums insist they be.) Ours are and they love it!

Letter writing is not easy to teach. If lessons are to have meaning, they should be tied to an ongoing activity. But often, when a related occasion arises, the children's interest doesn't run to letter writing—disinterest permeates the room when the words *format, style, capitalization, and punctuation* are mentioned.

To encourage interest in the skill, we revved up our imaginations and devised some thought-provoking (well … sometimes silly) letter-writing situations. That's how the following letter units, which we use throughout the year, came into being. We kept them short and to the point. Each described a situation, gave a sample reply, and was followed by an assignment.

Once the students got their feet wet with the first unit, they were eager—or, at least, willing—for more.

Now that we've started you on the road to renewing the art of letter writing, get at it *today!* It's as good a time as any.

Very truly yours,

Birute Gudauskas

James Charnock

P.S. We've done the work for you. Just reproduce the following pages, and use them when needed—school work or homework. You will, of course, instruct the class as to the exact placement and the proper number of spaces between parts.

Letter 1

Name_____ **Date** _____

You are watching the TV news when you hear that your favorite TV character, Commander Koenig, was hurt while filming a show about saving Moon Base Alpha from a galaxy of anti-matter globules. He is now in the hospital. Concerned, you write a **get-well** note.

> 24 South Street
> Hanover, PA 17331
> January 2, 2000

Dear Commander Koenig:
    I am writing to tell you that I think you are still the greatest! I only hope you will be feeling better soon.

> Most sincerely,
> *Johnny Jones*

Assignment 1: While crossing the street with you, one of your favorite friends is struck by an automobile. Your friend's left leg is broken, but, fortunately, the accident will not be crippling. Write a **get-well** note.

Letter 2

Name_____ Date _____

Yesterday your mother brought home an antique lamp. While pretending you were Commander Koenig, fighting off the invaders who had taken over Alpha's life-support system, you break it. Quickly you write a letter of **apology.**

January 3, 2005

Dear Mom,

I'm really sorry I broke your lamp. I shouldn't have been so careless. I have some money saved to pay for another lamp. It's not enough but take the rest out of my allowance for the next ten years.

Your loving son,
Johnny Jones

Assignment 2: On the first day of your vacation with your grandmother, she asks you to please not ride your bike on the newly seeded lawn. But one day you're late for dinner and you decide to carefully ride across the lawn. As you put on the brakes, a surprising skid tears up a patch of lawn. Write a letter of **apology.**

Letter 3

Name_____ **Date** _____

    It's your birthday and you've just opened a present from your "favorite" aunt. It's a hand-tooled leather belt with an ornamental buckle. (She's also the aunt who keeps reminding you to pull up your pants—no matter what the style is.) With gratitude and politeness, you write a **thank-you** letter.

February 3, 2005

My dear Aunt,

    Thank you very much for the leather belt. Wow, what a buckle! It's just exactly what I've always wanted.

Your nephew,
Johnny

Assignment 3: Another relative gives you educational gifts. When your mother writes that you're doing great in school, she rushes out and buys you a whole pack of pencils. Write a **thank-you** letter.

Letter 4

Name_____ **Date** _____

You are president of the South Street Moon Base Alpha Fan Club. You've just learned that you might be voted out of office at the next election. You're desperate and decide to do some electioneering. So you write an **invitation.**

March 7, 2005

Dear Moon Base Alpha Members:

As president of the South Street Chapter I invite you to my house for a pre-election party, Saturday, March 28, at 11 AM. Please try to make it.

A loyal fan,
Johnny Jones

R.S.V.P
24 South St.
Hanover, PA

Assignment 4: A new student has just arrived in your class and you want him to feel welcomed. Your parents agreed to a welcoming party on Friday or Saturday night. Write an **invitation.**

Letter 5

Name_____ **Date** _____

You've just spent the weekend with friends of your parents. Their daughter was a terrible pest. But her mother was a fantastic cook. When home, you write a **bread-and-butter** letter (a thanks for hospitality).

> 24 South Street
> Hanover, PA 17331
> April 3, 2005

Dear Mr. and Mrs. Brown,
Thank you very much for a nice weekend. You have a very charming daughter. Please send my mother your lemon-meringue pie recipe. I thought it was great!

> Thank you again,
> *Johnny Jones*

Assignment 5: While on a scouting trip you became friends with another scout. He invited you for a weekend at his home in the country. You had a fantastic time. Write a **bread-and-butter** letter for his and his family's hospitality.

Letter 6

Name_____ **Date** _____

Remember that fantastic pack of pencils from your relative? You'd like to repay her with an equally "lovely" present. You've found the perfect gift: A hand-crocheted doorknob cover. You write a **business** letter.

24 South Street
Hanover, PA 17331
March 1, 2005

Little Bit Gift Shop
2435 East Broad Street
Philadelphia, PA 19128

Dear Sir/Madam:

Will you please send me one hand-crocheted doorknob cover. I enclose a money order that includes the cost of shipping and handling.

Sincerely,
Johnny Jones
Johnny Jones

Assignment 6: Order the paperback edition of *Harry Potter and the Chamber of Secrets* by J. K. Rawling from Borders Books, 1001 Baltimore Pike, Springfield, PA 19064. The cost—including tax and shipping—is $8.85.

Letter 7

Name_____ **Date** _____

    You are away at summer camp and you're the oldest there. The mosquitoes like you but you're not too sure about the kids. You're miserable. Thinking about your envious friends at home you write a **friendly** letter.

> Beaver Camp
> Poultney, Vermont, 05741
> May 20, 2005

Dear Friends,
    I am having a fantastic time. This place is terrific! I wish *you* were here.

> Your friend,
> *Johnny*

Assignment 7: You are staying with your aunt, uncle, and cousins in the mountains. You are really getting to be a mountaineer. You go barefoot every day, drink tea made from a bush's root, and take an exciting canoe trip. Write your parents.

Letter 8

Name_____ **Date** _____

Your cousin Al won a goldfish-swallowing contest while being initiated into a college fraternity. Write a letter of **congratulations.**

June 5, 2005

Hi Al,

Congratulations on getting accepted into the fraternity. I know you have to have excellent marks to become and remain a member. Since you're the smartest relative I have, you probably won't get kicked out of the "club."

Your cousin,
Johnny

P.S. Do goldfish tickle going down?

Assignment 8: Your other cousin, Fred, is in the army. He did so well on an officer-candidate examination they sent him to West Point! He's just graduated as a second lieutenant. Write, congratulating him. (Add a "P.S."—postscript.)

Chapter 5

Classroom Interviewing

The Ground Rules

[This whole chapter is for reproduction.]

First, choose a partner to interview who, in turn, will interview you. But before going any further, each of you must write *at least* ten questions you would like the other to answer about him/herself.

There may not be enough class time today for the both of you to interview each other. Whether or not there is time, your assignment will be collected and handed back to you as soon as possible so you can finish.

To get a feel for what is expected of you, we will read and discuss the two interview styles accompanying this paper before you start—more about style, later.

The Interview

In all interviewing you don't *just* ask prepared questions. Observe your partner's behavior and reaction to your questions and write that down too (you may use it later). Try to "draw out" your partner/interviewee by asking him or her to elaborate. And don't be shy to react to any answers or ask unprepared and fol-low-up questions.

Note that the interviewee does not have to answer a question just because you ask.

Some Ideas

Following are some suggested areas from which you might draw to ask your questions:

1. Hobbies

2. Trips

3. After-school activities

4. Short-range goals

5. Long-range goals

6. Hardships (problems) expected to face in the future

7. Hardships faced in the past

8. What the person is reasonably good at doing (basket-ball, drawing, etc.)

9. Fear that might be admitted

10. Feelings about a current, controversial, or newswor-thy subject

11. What issue(s) the person has strong ideas about

12. Allowance and how it's spent

13. School subjects loved and hated

14. Home chores

15. Siblings

16. Person's good points and admitted failures or weak-nesses

17. Things one has to do but hates

After the Interview

After each interview, each of you will *separately* write a rough draft. Each of you is permitted to see what the other has written in order to correct any inaccuracies. The final draft should be agreed upon by both of you. (There should be no surprises.)

You, also, must write the interview in *both* of the styles as in the examples supplied here. Do the question-and-answer format first. When that is handed in and checked for quality (maybe in consultation with you), it will be handed back to you to use as an aid or memory-jogger to help you write the interview in the paragraph style.

Finally, after *all* drafts have been handed in and returned to you, you must orally present your interviewee to the class by telling what you learned about him or her—without reading from your written interview. (You may have already known some of this information before the interview, but everyone else doesn't.)

An Interview with Barbara Wyncote

By Mr. Charnock

(Style 1: Question-and-Answer)

Charnock: What do you like about being a junior high student at Ellsworth School?

Barbara: I don't like it that we don't change classes as is done in other junior highs.

Charnock: Isn't there something you like?

Barbara: I like the projects—like going downstairs and reading.

Charnock: What would you say you are good at in school?

Barbara: I'm good at writing. And also literature and reading.

Charnock: You get good grades in those subjects?

Barbara: Yeah.

Charnock: What do you think you will do as an adult; your career?

Barbara: Probably be a writer or lawyer—a prosecutor of criminals—to put those rats in jail where they belong.

Charnock: What are your hobbies; things you enjoy doing after school or on weekends?

Barbara: Play football.

Charnock: Touch football?

Barbara: Yeah.

Charnock: Anything else?

Barbara: Baseball. I'm going to play for the Rockport team.

Charnock: Isn't that for Rockport residents?

Barbara: Well, I'm going to visit with [a relative] in Rockport and they won't know I'm not from Rockport.

Charnock: How about some non-sport interests?

Barbara: *I have* to listen to the radio. *All* the time. *I need* it.

Charnock: What do you listen to?

Barbara: Rap music and rock-'n'-roll. I listen to them when I'm studying; all the time. Then there's the arcade.

Charnock: Pinball machines?

Barbara: Video.

Charnock: What school do you hope to attend next year?

Barbara: Johnson High.

Charnock: Why?

Barbara: They have both good nursing and scholastic programs.

Comments

The above style is verbatim conversation; in other words, quotes. It is slower to read than the paragraphed interview below. Additionally, I hope you sensed that there is room for improvement while still being true to the verbatim, question-and-answer format. For example, after Barbara told me what school she planned to attend, I did not have to slow the reader down by injecting "Charnock: Why?" I could have simply added her *answer* as a continuation of her previous statement since they go together. Please remember to do that in your assignment.

(Style 2: Paragraphing)

Barbara has mixed feeling about being in junior high at Ellsworth School. Although she enjoys participating in some unusual projects like storytaking and storyreading with primary students, she would like to change classes for different subjects as is done in other junior highs.

She spoke with confidence about her ability to write—maybe her primary academic interest—as well as read and report on literature. She reports good grades in these areas. At present, her future interests are journalism and a career in criminal law. She wants to "put those rats [criminals] in jail where they belong."

On the non-academic side, Barbara did not seem the slightest bothered by enjoying some sports that most girls shun—or, as usual, only participate in as spectators. She plays touch football when the season is in. And, this summer, hopes to play on a Rockport baseball team—even if she has to pretend she lives in Rockport, not Framingham. When these activities are not available, there are always the arcade, video games and the like.

Although she gave the appearance of being quite independent, Barbara did admit to being enslaved to one thing: the radio. She *"needs"* it, she said. "It" being rock-'n'-roll and rap.

Next year it may be Johnson High School. She's impressed with the school's scholastic and nursing programs. (So, now it's lawyer, journalist … or nurse.)

Comments

Using the paragraph style you can choose to quote when you think it effective. You can also put in more of your interpretation or feeling into the interview write-up. This may be a more difficult style of writing for you, but it is a skill you need to practice. Your previous assignment should help.

Chapter 6

The Art of Story*taking*

You say you're overcome with grief? That your students don't recognize sentences? Can't punctuate, capitalize, or spell? That you find teaching such skills boring—both for you and your students? W-e-l-l, look no further, friend. I have here a sure cure for what ails you. Your students will learn how to recognize written sentences, punctuate, capital-ize, spell, and pick up a little grammar to boot. And all this elixir of pain will cost you is your misery. It's more than worth it, my friend: You'll get back many times your investment in pleasure and student learning. All I ask is that you give it a try. Your satisfaction is guaranteed or your misery back.

No, I'm not selling the equivalent of snake oil, but the idea that the learner learns best who is totally involved in a purposeful and enjoyable task. Student storytaking (an older student writing down the dictated story of a younger one) seems to possess just the right combination of elements to make it one of the best tools for basic language skills learning, pleasing all concerned: structure and creativity, teacher control and independence, indi-vidual initiative and collaboration, challenge and reward.

Because I have found student storytaking one of the best ways to instill and reinforce the aforementioned writing and spelling skills, I feel bound to share my experience with this technique with you. As this chapter unfolds you will be able to see how the combination of personal dynamics in a storytaking program works, and, I hope, sense the excitement and learning such a program engenders.

First I will tell you what I have found helpful in preparing my students, the cooperating teachers, and myself for this venture. Then I will supply you with the basic information each storytaker needs to know. These suggestions are offered to enhance student and teacher interest and feelings of confidence and competence.

Mechanics of Writing

One of several reasons for a storytaking program is to increase the student storytakers' skill in recognizing sentences in their writing. Unless they are made more aware, the sentence punctuation and capitalization they neglect in their own generated sentences they will also neglect in taking dictation. A sure, non-drudgery way to increase skillfulness in recognizing sentences in writing is to acquaint the student with the *hearing* of them; that is, the student should be attuned to the sound pattern that ends a sentence: basically, the pause. Of course, a comma pause and a period pause cannot always be distinguished, but at this stage of writing development such a distinction is not all that important.

The teaching of this skill—so that all that is involved in a storytaking assignment will not become onerous—can be done in the following way:

1. Type up about fifteen paragraphs with about five short sentences each from various books or juvenile

magazines with a reading level that is easy for all—but leave out the sentence punctuation and capitalization, including any hint of the between-sentence spacing.

2. Duplicate a copy for each student. Daily or frequently read three short paragraphs for the students as they listen and read silently along. Read each paragraph three times in the manner in which the author wrote it. The students are to listen for the pauses and punctuate what they hear. Then after each paragraph, and with a partner, each can compare (debate/correct) the other's interpretations. Next, read the paragraph to them, telling where the periods and sentence and perhaps other capitalization go.

You may wish to incidentally point out some of the more obvious times when a comma is used: with appositives, interjections, some clauses and phrases, words in a series, direct address, and others you feel important. But if you overdo this aspect, you will kill interest.

I have found this practice is enough to start the storytakers on their way to the mechanics of storytaking. This practice, nevertheless, needs to be reinforced when each student consults you or your aide before writing the story into booklet form to return to the story*teller.* This can be done by having the student quietly read the dictated story aloud. In this way students will often catch (hear) their silent-reading failure to punctuate (and often capitalize). But when they don't, have them re-read that line to find the period or obvious comma.

The Logistics

I send two to four students every week to each cooperating primary-grade teacher's room. (Sometimes I deal only with one teacher at a time so my program doesn't stretch out too long.) The first storytaking visit lasts about a half-hour, the second return trip about fifteen minutes.

Volunteers, to get the program started, are fine at first, but a schedule is necessary to keep track of who is going, when, where, and how often. I ask the cooperating teacher to send these students to separate parts of the room so they won't disturb each other and the class—and also to lessen shyness or self-consciousness in performing in close proximity to others. (The librarian may agree to accept such pairs, too.)

I try to send students to different rooms for subsequent storytaking assignments— assuming we're not dealing with just one teacher.

My students, fifth through eighth graders, storytake in grades one through three—in the latter part of the year a kindergarten teacher may request my students' "services."

A cautionary note: Storytakers sometimes forget to finish the job before their follow-up visit if they have to put their draft aside when returning to class, which they must do in my class. So, you will have to set a definite time for them to finish the assignment in school or at home and then consult you. Otherwise, they may not be able to keep to the scheduled revisiting time, and this will not sit well with the cooperating teacher.

Motivation

Encourage the students to be very polite to the cooperating teacher; otherwise, they may jeopardize the program in that teacher's room for following students. They should not converse with students when entering or leaving the room. If the cooperating teacher wrongly accuses them of making noise, for example, they should just take it.

On the more positive side, let them know that the primary grade children will delight in getting special attention. That these smaller students will look upon them, the storytakers, as important people. In addition, it will be a fun time as well as a time of learning for both.

Although I will instruct the entire class about the details of our storytaking program, I–or a competent aide—will meet with the storytakers just prior to their very first visit in the program, and their first return visit, to go over the details again and to insure their interest. Once this has been done for all new storytakers, I have only to consult with them before they prepare their booklets on subsequent visits—in order to check on mechanics, spelling, and grammar (most teachers expect that).

Qualifications

Let your class know that a reasonable skill in reading (which is often reflected in writing or spelling) is needed for storytaking. Therefore, only students reading at grade four and above may participate. Nevertheless, I have sent very motivated third-grade readers and not allowed some grade-four-and-above readers to participate who were very indifferent; the latter a rare occurrence. Basically, though, this is not a volunteer program, but is considered as part of the students' language skills learning. In spite of this matter-of-fact stance, I have never had a student, once started, request to drop out of the program.

Preparing the Cooperating Teacher and Yourself

Some teachers will accept the idea of having storytakers in their room with enthusiasm, others with caution. Because of this natural range of feelings, the cautious members can be asked if they would like to *try* the idea for a week, then make a decision. Make sure you send to such a teacher your most cooperative, personable, and academically skilled students.

For all teachers set a limit for the program—two or three months—so they will not feel prisoner to your idea. At the end of this period actually end the program, but inform the teachers that should they want you to resume sometime in the future you will be glad to. Responses to this "out" (when it comes) may range from "I don't want you to stop" to "Maybe it'd be nice to continue in the spring" to an indefinite "Okay" and a thanks.

Explain to the teachers the benefits of your program to the both of you. (I think it is best to do this on a one-to-one basis rather than through a faculty meeting.) The other teachers' students should acquire additional sight vocabulary (their own words), learn sound-spelling correspondences, help build a library of student-generated booklets, grow in appreciating the writing side of language, and enjoy the public sharing of an experience.

Your students will reinforce their knowledge of sentence mechanics and capitalization—and the concept of sentencing, in general—as well as their knowledge of paragraphing. They will put to practice what they have been taught about phonics, learn to spell a little better, acquire some sight vocabulary, and deal with their own and another's non-standard usages. In addition you'll have a means of informal but sufficient evaluation of the students' literacy skills.

And all this learning will be packaged in the enjoyable mode of storytaking.

So that the teachers will understand and appreciate your program more, give them a copy of the information supplied to the storytakers (at the end of this chapter).

Request that the cooperating teachers start the storytakers off with some of their more academically skilled and verbose students so everyone, all around, will feel successful in this venture from the very beginning. This will have a positive effect in launching the program.

There will be one story*teller* per story*taker.*

Although you will have your own convictions about how much to correct or not correct a storyteller's (dictated) language and a storytaker's writing, it will probably be best to consult the wishes of the cooperating teacher. Most will probably desire that the more non-standard usages be changed by the storytaker and writer (and you), and that spelling be reasonably, if not entirely, correct.

Try, for your own sanity and educational program, to set up a common time and day(s) between you and the cooperating teacher(s) for when the storytakers can visit. Mine visit at 1:30 p.m. when I have a daily half-hour silent-reading period. The storytakers hate to miss this time, but since each only storytakes once every three weeks, they can bear it. Additionally, they are not missing direct instruction. You will have to discover the time/s and days best for you and the cooperating teacher.

The most difficult part of your program may be in finding the time to consult with the students to check their rewrite of their story/dictation-taking. I—or a qualified aide—quietly consult with such students, one-to-one, during Silent Reading Period when some are reading and some are off taking stories.

The unimproved story or its improved draft (on lined paper) is kept in a file, in front of my desk, behind the storytaker's name. It stays there and is retrieved from there until it is finished and suitable to present back to the story*teller.* After the text has been approved, the student can put it into booklet form between attractive covers.

Storytaking Instructions

The "Student Storytaking" instructions, at the end of this chapter, can be distributed to the students and explained to them. Each student can keep a copy in his or her writing folder or place it in a notebook for future reference. (Run off extra sheets because up to one-fourth the class will lose the information.)

> *Step right up, folks, and try this surefire approach. Have faith in its success. It's worked wonders for others; it can do so for you. (Uh ... don't forget to deposit your misery as you leave.) Thank you, one and all!*

STUDENT STORYTAKING

How to Start

1. Introduce yourself to the student and get his or her name.

2. Tell what is going to happen: The student will tell you something and you will write it down so s/he can show it to others—the teacher, other students, and his or her parents.

3. Use manuscript writing—that's all this student may know.

4. Take several lined sheets of paper and a pen or two sharpened pencils

The Procedure

1. Have the storyteller sit *beside* you so s/he can see you write his words as they are being said.

2. Skip lines so that if the student wants to change something, or you want to make corrections, there is space to do this.

3. As the student is recalling or inventing a story, feed him/her questions to get a more elaborate tale. You don't want a skeleton of a story, but a full one. Also, keep the student to the topic—or *purposely* make several subtopics.

4. After the student has dictated the story to you, read it back to him—using your finger as you read—while the storyteller visually follows along. In fact, tell him/her to do this.

5. Let the student change (revise) part of the story if s/he wants. You should make this point early in your dictation taking.

6. Read the story you've taken back to the student the best you can. This will help you and the teller iron out any "bugs."

7. Take this first draft back to the room and place it in your folder in the "Storytaking File." Be sure the child's and teacher's names and the room number are on the paper—as well as your name—just in case you're absent and a substitute needs to take your place and finish the job.

8. Now, you have to write a second draft as well as you can. *This* product will receive a grade. You may take it home to complete or work on it during Silent Reading Period.

9. Next, meet with me to check your copy before you write it into a booklet.

10. After approval, you can make your storybook. A supply of 4-1/2"x7" lined pages and construction paper covers will be in the Storytaking File. When writing, besides being neat, be sure to leave a one-finger-wide margin on the right side of the page and a two-finger margin on the left (for stapling). Use only a pencil with No. 2 lead so you can neatly erase mistakes. Capitalize all important words on the story's title page and underline it. Be sure to print in *manuscript* style.

11. Underneath the title write the "by" line (by Johnny Williams, for example). Next, skip a line and start the story, being sure to indent the first line and the first line of every paragraph/subtopic. Skip lines to take up space and make the booklet look fuller. Finally, you can make the cover pretty by writing the title and by-line with crayon, colored pencil, or magic marker and decorating the cover with pictures related to the story. At the bottom of the cover write "Storytaker: Your Name."

12. See me for a final check.

13. Return the story to the student, as scheduled, and re-read it to him/her. If able, have the student read it back to you, helping him or her along the way.

14. Give the storybook to the student to give to his teacher, who may read it to the class—or let the student do so—and post it on the bulletin board for others to see or place in a student-generated library for others to borrow and read. (I'm sure his or her parents will eventually get it.)

Your Behavior

1. Don't criticize the storyteller. In fact, try to find something nice to say about his or her story. If the story doesn't make sense to you, say you don't understand and ask for that part to be repeated differently. If this doesn't work, just let it stand. If the child can't think of anything to say, even after you've offered ideas, then politely ask the teacher if you can have another student, but thank this one for trying, adding that he or she will have another chance later.

2. Talk quietly at all times.

3. Follow all the cooperating teacher's instructions.

4. Quietly thank the student when finished and the teacher as you leave—unless a thank-you to the teacher would interrupt her. A wave and a smile would then be sufficient.

Storytaking Ideas

1. You can tell me about anything you want.

2. Tell me about a trip you took.

3. Would you like to tell me a make-believe story?

4. Can you remember one time when you were scared? What happened?

5. Do you have a favorite fun activity? What is it?

6. Do you have a job around the house? Tell me about it.

7. Come up with your own questions.

(Remember, if you feel the child's story is much too short or unclear in spots, get him or her to elaborate by asking questions one after another so more details will be revealed.)

(Example Letter & Scheduling Form for Cooperating Teacher)

Dear Colleagues,

As per our conversation about our Storytaking Program, my students are eager to start. They have been learning about the program and practicing skills needed for it to be successful for both your students and mine.

Please indicate below the number of students who may be sent to your room at one time and the days and time(s) they may visit.

(Remember, a student will visit to take a story, person-to-person, then return when the booklet is complete.)

Sincerely,

James Charnock

James Charnock, RM. 309

Storytaking Program Schedule

Teacher_____

\# of Students _____Room # _____

Days Available	Times Available
Monday	_____
Tuesday	_____
Wednesday	_____
Thursday	_____
Friday	_____

STORYTAKING PROGRAM

Week of_____

DAY	TIME	TEACHER/RM	GRADE	STORY*TAKER*

Note to teacher: Fill in after consulting teacher/s. Change weekly. Use more than one row if more than two students are visiting a room. To add color: scan and print title in bold red, column headings in bold blue. Can photocopy enlarge if needed.

Chapter 7

LINE UP!

A Game, Not a Command

At first, I thought I would start this chapter with a little pizzazz:

> *Punctuation and capitalization that's not drudgery—to you and your students! That's what LINE UP! promises. LINE UP!, an exciting whole-class game, will make basic sentence capitalization and punctuation unforgettable. Students will remember what they are "taught" because they are energetically involved. Experience LINE UP! and prove to yourself and your students that here is one subject that isn't what it used to be.*

On second thought, the following seemed a little more level-headed:

> *In an atmosphere of cooperation, competition, and challenge, your students can reinforce essential sentence capitalization and punctuation skills without being tediously aware of how much they are learning. LINE UP!——a mentally, physically, and socially active game—creates such an atmosphere and an enthusiastic response from both*

player and classroom audience. Whether your students are average, mentally gifted, or slow in acquiring academic skills, LINE UP! will prove exciting and beneficial—even to those who usually consider acquiring and sharpening sentence mechanics a dull routine.

But, as you can see, the chapter starts somewhere in-between:

How many times have you had to "shush" a student playing an exciting language arts game in the corner of the room—if you *have* an *exciting* language arts game? Well, with LINE UP! students can let it all out and with your approval and at your direction. No more shushing. In fact, you had better close the door to keep the noise of excitement inside the room. (No, that's not an exaggeration.)

Not only will the structured chaos (sounds contradictory, doesn't it?) of the game thrill the participants, but you'll observe in the classroom audience anticipation (*When* will I get in to play?), frustration (How could she make *that* mistake?), attempts at cheating (No, it goes over *here!*), and support (*Hurry up*, Team Two!).

The "Theory" Behind LINE UP!

LINE UP! lets you in on the fun. That's part of its purpose. You direct the game, score the points (though a student may register them at the chalkboard), keep the excitement and rules of the game in hand, and laugh along with your students.

The players are totally engaged: mentally (or cognitively, if you prefer), physically (they won't have to sit still—whether active participants or active viewers), and socially (the cooperation, competition, and demonstration in front of their peers is just plain fun). In fact, they are involved in the process of reinforcing essential sentence mechanics skills without being tediously aware of how much they are learning. And we've all known for some time that a child learns more, and more efficiently, the greater the number of senses s/he uses while learning.

Interest is maintained by the fact that the game is not made too easy. Otherwise it would quickly lose its appeal. Players are forced to think. For instance (and depending upon the game version), whether to use jack or Jack; girl's, girls', or girls; where to place the quotation marks; how to translate the *manner* in which you dictate the sentence by the use of appropriate punctuation— and more.

The red color for punctuation marks and capitalized letters is a distinct advantage of the game's visual approach both for the players and the audience: It helps use another of the senses to reinforce the concepts being learned or reinforced.

How Much Skill Is Needed to Play the Game?

A little. Obviously a child can't place a punctuation mark if he doesn't know what it is or hasn't seen it in use or practiced using it in writing. Likewise, for capitals.

But once this initial familiarity is established by you, the game will serve its intended function: to reinforce sentence capitalization and punctuation concepts in an involving way.

This Game Is Competitive. Does It Have a Cooperative or Affective Element?

You bet. Cross-team competition requires in-team cooperation. Less skilled students are aided by the more skilled to help the whole team.

In addition, active participation can be voluntary. Often, shy and very sensitive students willingly participate when they see this in-team relationship, and that they can get an easier team "job" of placing a dictated non-capitalized word rather than a punctuation symbol or capitalized word.

Of course, it's important for you to set the tone (the spirit of cooperation) in the play of the game.

For What Grades or Ages Is LINE UP! Suited?

Depending on the version of the game and the skill of your students, LINE UP! is suitable for grades two through six—but, not surprisingly, seventh and eighth graders thoroughly enjoy LINE UP! too! Include also the educable mentally retarded in the intermediate (grades four through six) through eighth grade range.

There Are Teams. Why No Team Captains?

First of all, if you exercise the option to enhance total class participation (that is, the possibility of audience members actively entering the game) by sitting down those who cause minus points for their team by penalty or mistake, maintaining a captain will be a cumbersome task: The captain will have to sit down from time to time, and thus a new captain found—and so it will go.

Secondly, and most importantly, a captain will make the game too orderly, cause less thinking on the part of some team members (because they're being told what to do), and help erase some of the chaos and confusion—taking away all the fun!

Additionally, a captain may tend to make the game too competitive.

Of course, if an informal, non-appointed "leader" emerges during play, this shouldn't be discouraged—but the members are not obliged to submit to his or her directions.

There're Only Ten Sentences. Won't the Students Get Bored?

Perhaps only Popeye could eat spinach daily and relish it. So don't overdo it: About once every week or two and no more. You want to keep interest in the game high so you can use it as an effective, involving reinforcement.

You'll find that limiting play to five sentences at a time will be quite enough to whet the students' appetites, but only that. Leave them hungry for the next time. Five sentences will take twenty minutes or more.

Students will not become bored with "only" ten sentences because their main concentration is on the mechanics of sentencing and not the particular words or sequence of words. Thus, they do not remember the sentence next time around. The element of racing to be the first team lined up helps assure this.

Is LINE UP! Really Only a Whole-Class Game?

Although LINE UP! is primarily designed for whole-class use (teacher, players and audience), once it is understood, it can be played by as few as two students. Instead of holding up the cards, the pupils can simply place them in order on a big table or on the carpet or floor.

How Is the Game Constructed?

Each game version has duplicate sets of word and punctuation-symbol cards. The color of each set is slightly different so that the cards of one set will not be confused with the other.

The "Key Card" gives you the sentences for dictating as well as the list and number of all words and symbols used.

Note that all sentences contain the same total number of words and punctuation symbols.

All letters, except capitalized letters, are printed in blue. Capital letters and punctuation marks are printed in red.

What Equipment Is Needed?

You will need two large tables (or two groups of four desks)—one for each team—to place, separated, at the end of the room. If you don't have tables or suitable desks, any sizable flat surface works well: windowsill and so on.

How Is the Game Played?

Separate the game version's duplicate cards to form two identical sets—one for each of the two teams. Place the cards, face-up, on each team's table. (Each team's capitalized, non-capitalized, and punctuation cards can be placed into separate columns if you find this facilitates play.)

Direct the forming of the two teams, balancing them skill-wise as much as possible. (The number on each team is equal to the number of word and symbol cards per sentence; that is, six or eight, depending on the game version used.)

When play starts for each sentence, team members quietly stand around their respective table with hands behind their backs while you read a sentence from the Key Card *twice*—with the vocal inflection dictated by the punctuation. If any of the players reach for a card before the *end* of the second reading, the player's team is penalized one point for each violation. After the round starts, you can repeat the sentence when requested.

The team goal is to consistently be the first to line up in front of their table (facing the class and you) with each member holding one of the cards to form your dictated sentence—with capitalized words and punctuation symbols properly placed.

During play, if a team lines up incorrectly, your response to them should not reveal the type of mistake they have made, but, at most, the number of mistakes in the sentence. So, they will have to continue "struggling" to get it right.

When one team finishes a sentence correctly, you will call "Freeze!" Each team's players must then freeze in place or the team is penalized one point (or one point for each "non-freezer"—it's up to you).

The winning team for that round (sentence) receives the number of total points per sentence—which is the total number of cards in the sentence—less any penalty. The losing team has points subtracted from the sentence for each mistake or omission plus any penalty.

Sometimes it happens that the losing team lines up correctly just as you call freeze, but after you have recognized that the opposing team is already properly in their positions. In this case simply subtract one point from the losing team's total for that sentence or round.

At this point, those members of each team who were responsible for subtracted points may be replaced by other classroom members in order to enhance total class participation and interest. This is optional on your part because it will depend upon whether you and/or the students consider this practice beneficial to the spirit and play of the game. (It could become cumbersome.) With this approach, retiring players have a chance to re-enter the game.

If a sentence appears too difficult to construct, you may want to call "Freeze!" or ask the players if they wish to freeze (they often insist on continuing), score the number of correct positions for each team, and then go on. You should, of course, demonstrate how the sentence should have been formed.

The audience and players should be made aware that while the team members may help each other, coaching (and seeking coaching—a penalty point) from the audience is prohibited. And that an audience member at fault may be penalized by not being chosen as a replacement, if you so decide.

You will have to determine whether to use more than five sentences in the play of the game. Though five sentences seem quite sufficient, the students' level of enthusiasm, skill, and the available time will probably help dictate your decision. Regardless, the team with the highest score at the end of play is the winner.

FACSIMILE CARD SAMPLES

(Use oaktag and laminate for durability)

<u>Key Card</u>

Game Version #1 (Grades 2-4)

(front)

<table>
<tr><td>

<u>Concept Concentration:</u>
1. Capitalization
   a. Sentence opening
   b. Proper name
2. Punctuation
   a. Comma: direct address, pause
   b. Sentence closings: period, question
     and explanation marks

</td><td>

<u>Capitals:</u>
Bill, Come, Does, Jack,
  Please, Quickly, The,
  Will, Yes (9+9 cards)
<u>Smalls:</u>
  bill, come, hand, here,
  jack, look, please,
  quickly, the, today, will,
  well, you (13+13 cards)
<u>Punctuation:</u> **!/./?/,**
(4+4 Cards)
<u>Players:</u> 6+6
<u>Total Cards:</u>
(26+26)+2=54

</td></tr>
</table>

FACSIMILE CARD SAMPLES

(Use oaktag and laminate for durability)

Key Card

Game Version #1 (Grades 2-4)

(back)

Sentences for Dictation:
1. Yes, Bill will come.
2. Come here quickly, Jack!
3. The bill will come today.
4. Please hand Bill the jack.
5. Will you look, please?

6. Quickly hand Jack the jack!
7. Does Jack look well today?
8. Please, will you come?
9. Bill, you look well.
10. Jack, please look here!

For easier learning I suggest you write/print the capital letters and punctuation marks in bold red and the other letters in bold blue; they are in bold black herein.

Below are other versions/concept concentrations of LINE UP! Just remember that *each* word and *each* punctuation mark has its own 3 x 9-inch rectangular card and the mechanics emphasized (capital letters; quotation, exclamation and punctuation marks; apostrophes and commas) are in red.

Game Version #2 (Grades 2-6)

Concept Concentration: Apostrophe of Possession Sentences for Dictation:

1 The girl's pets are good.
2 Are the boys hurt outside?
3. Don't hurt the dog's paw!
4. Is the car's door open?
5. He lost the boy's car.

6. Your girls are hurt outside!
7. Your dogs are very good.
8. The pet's paw is hurt.
9. The cars are very good.
10. The girls' coats are good.

Game Version #3 (Grades 2/3-6)

Concept Concentration: Direct Quotes Sentences for Dictation:

1. Bill shouted, "Come here!"
2. "He came," answered Joe.
3. "Are you?" asked Mary.
4. Bill asked, "Whose book?"
5. "I came," Mary said.

6. "Why you?" Joe asked.
7. Bill answered, "I see."
8. Joe shouted, "How come!"
9. "Come here," Mary said.
10. "Go inside!" shouted Bill.

A final reminder: Make two cards (one for each of the two teams) of each *different* word and punctuation mark. Count the number of words and marks in a sentence and that is the number of students on each team. For Version #3, above, that's eight students per team.

Bill	?	bill

Chapter 8

"Doing" a Poem:

"The Lurpp is on the Loose"

or

How to Start Losing Your Fear of Classroom Drama

If you are like me, you are probably a little scared to engage your students in classroom dramatics. Of course, if you are a kindergarten or first-grade teacher, most would, traditionally, expect you to be more or less expert at this sort of thing; but a fifth- or sixth-grade teacher?

Scared? Well, let us say so unsure of our own and our students' abilities that we never take a story, poem, or idea and turn it into a skit or play. Yet, behind this wall of a fear of failure is a desire to succeed at just this very thing—because the students obviously enjoy learning and sharing in this way.

Did I say learning? Yes. What better way to do "interpretive" (inferential, main idea, drawing conclusions) and "creative" type thinking than to translate an idea, poem, or story into a dramatic presentation. Personally experiencing the mood, motives, plot, and characterizations of a narrative or situation surely gets across these ideas vividly to students who are expected to enjoy them in their personal and critical reading and use them when writing. Since they have "been there," they know more about it.

Though I had been on the outside looking in for years (reading articles, hearing speeches, and watching other teachers' students), I had almost never gotten into the action of using dramatics in my classroom. I had my rationalizations, of course: the time involved, student (mis)behavior, a lack of student talent or ability, a meager output for the effort of input, and, unadmitted, the lack of confidence in myself. The latter was probably the real reason; the former just excuses.

It may take a total of a few hours (stretched out over a week or two) to "perfect" a ten-minute skit for presentation to others. Is it worth it? Consider that we have probably involved at least a third or more of our class, and all attention-wise, to the possibilities that lie within an idea, a situation, or a poem. They will see or experience many of those skills we have been trying to get across in other ways with sometimes-meager results. There will be creativity but within the recognizable structure of the story. Adaptation and interpretation (both in words and body movements) represent analytical thinking—something we are usually proud to display otherwise.

We are building within the students the potential for future dramatic interpretations and sharing by demonstrating the possibilities that this one piece of literature (or what have you) can offer. We may need or want to lead them down the road the first time or two, but they will soon want to become independent and assertive if they can see we are willing to step aside and just walk with them.

With reference to behavior, admittedly, some classes are better than others either because of our management skills, teaching techniques, or personality. Most likely we are not going to undergo a personality change so the students can experience dramatics (since we may feel they are acting up enough as it is). Our ability to manage or direct or "control" our students is, if our personality does not do it, greatly dependent upon our techniques in teaching. And here is where classroom drama can come to our aid as a technique that will foster not only the obvious curriculum but group cohesion, leadership, cooperation, and an acceptable way to "show off." This is not to say we will not have our problems with behavior: We may have to get angry and sit down students from time to time—even eliminate one from the action—but, all in all, we will be building momentum for the students' interest in learning and literature and, at the same time, building their confidence in our ability to guide them.

If we have never had our students demonstrate their understanding and appreciation of an idea, situation, or piece of literature by performing it, then there is no way we can know of their ability to do so. If we have had only one or two occasions over the years to witness what our pupils can do in this area, then the effort was probably more due to the students' initiative than to our encouragement. We will probably continue to have just as few experiences.

I was surprised at the ability of my students this year in performing (interpreting to some extent) the poem that accompanies this chapter. Some skill was obvious from the beginning; some developed through practice and performances. Self-confidence, in spite of fears, and pleasure increased and carried us forward.

The complaint that spending several classroom hours for a ten-minute product (and not all such activities will have this ratio) is an uneconomical use of instructional time needs to be addressed. But this is difficult to do because the results of such classroom activities are not easily measured or always fast in coming. We can understand how the underlying skills developed in preparing drama or in performing pantomime and improvisation can translate into or transfer to other language arts, but we have no objective tests to demonstrate this.

Nevertheless, those of us who use such excuses to avoid classroom drama probably engage in "approved" activities that produce even less demonstrable results for the amount of time spent on them: The constant review of grammar and sentence mechanics, literary "analysis," and undue emphasis on parts of speech. Even the sacrosanct teaching of spelling is not very efficient compared to the practical results.

Probably, though, at the heart of much non-participation is our lack of confidence in guiding the students into expressive efforts. Some of this can be attributed to our own personality, lack of experience, and the absence of learning in our college course work or school staff development. But much must be to our failure to simply wade into the water. Such water is frightening when we do not know how to swim; however, we have learned enough from experience, listening, reading, and watching to mimic the good swimmer. Like swimming, I am convinced that this is one activity that improves with practice.

At this point I would like to share with you a ten-minute drama activity our class performed this year. I hope it is only one of several to come. We performed it (as fifth and sixth graders) in the primary classrooms; in the classrooms mainly because I feel classroom performances are less frightening to the child than a distant, big audience. There is a more intimate relationship between performer and viewer, and the dramatists get to perform several times, which means they get to re-enjoy their success and improve their presentation and, thus, build confidence. If they flop once on the big stage, they have flopped for good.

The activity was a slightly changed poem by Jack Prelutsky (from *The Snopp on the Sidewalk and Other Poems*, New York, Greenwillow, 1977). We simply changed its number from the singular to the plural; thus, it was called "The Lurpps Are on the Loose." It is a monster poem that is really meant to be nonsensical, but it can be experienced with a pretense of the horrid. For reprint permission reasons, it is printed below as Jack Prelutsky wrote it; just remember to change "lurpp" to "Lurpps," "is" to "are," "It" to "They," and "It's" to "They're" when you use it with a group:

Oh the lurpp is on the loose, the loose,
the lurpp is on the loose.
It caused a fretful, frightful fuss
when it swallowed a ship and ate a bus
and now it's after all of us,
oh the lurpp is on the loose.

Oh the lurpp is on the loose, the loose,
the lurpp is on the loose.
It weighs about a zillion pounds,
it's making loud and lurppy sounds
as it follows us with bumbly bounds,
oh the lurpp is on the loose.

Oh the lurpp is on the loose, the loose,
the lurpp is on the loose.
It's covered with horns and thorns and claws
and razor teeth adorn its jaws,

so everyone's running away, because
the lurpp is on the loose.

When I first read this poem, I looked, as I always do with literature now, for a way to get it into the student's experience, a way to interpret it through an expressive art. I discovered three ways: drama (including choral speaking), music (a cappella singing), and art. Only secondarily did I speculate that we might share our adventure outside the classroom, as it so happened.

On the day of my presentation I prepared the atmosphere by pulling the shades and lighting several candles. I asked the students to imagine or remember a time when they were swept along by others who were terribly frightened by something or someone that they, themselves, had not yet seen or heard. Why would they believe these frightened people? Why would they start to feel and act like them? The poem, I told them dramatically, is about such a situation, and it involves m-o-n-s-t-e-r-s.

I read the poem through once in as mockingly serious a voice as I could muster. After my reading they realized that my concocted atmosphere was a little too dramatic for the sense of the poem, but they seemed to appreciate the contradiction since the poem itself presented a similar one.

On the second reading I asked them to pay special attention to the description of the monsters.

Next, I asked the children to repeat (echo) each line after each was read to them—and in the manner in which each was read. (Lines one and two of each stanza were combined.) I revealed a transparency of the poem on the overhead projector and asked the students to imagine themselves being part of a crowd on the edge of a town running to spread the horrible news of this frightening monster so others could escape with their lives. The size of the crowd increases as more and more people become scared and join them in fleeing and warning others.

This imagined mood was brought into their experience more fully by using cumulative grouping for each stanza reading, as follows:

> Lines 1, 2: Teacher (or student)
> Line 3: Group A and teacher
> Line 4: Groups A, B, and teacher
> Line 5: Groups A, B, C, and teacher
> Line 6: Groups A, B, C, D, and teacher

Eventually, I dropped out of the recitation.

Next, the nonsensicalness of the poem was increased by turning it into a mockingly who's-afraid-of-the-lurpps joyous song. This was sung a cappella. (Of course, if you are talented with a musical instrument, such accompaniment cannot help but be enjoyed.)

I took a few "serious" moments to ask them what they thought words like "fretful," "lurppy," "bounds," and "adorn" meant. Responses to this more typical approach did not require the typical probing.

Finally, the students engaged in what they seemed to consider the enjoyable task of drawing and coloring the worst-looking and scariest monster masks to fit the poem's description. Our ESL teacher had explained the poem to my students not yet proficient in English, who drew some very fascinating monsters.

It was at this time that I broached the possibility of "doing" the poem in the primary classrooms. The idea was enthusiastically accepted. Especially since some of the students would get to wear the masks to thoroughly frighten some of the little people. We voted on the most suitable masks for our presentations and I cut out eye and nose holes—often nowhere near the monster's features. (Later, most masks got displayed on the hall bulletin board along with the poem and some snapshots.)

This was the point where the real work began. I used a cassette recorder to show the students how they were not together when reciting and singing, how they slurred over words or were less dramatic in voice than they could be. This helped—they liked hearing themselves on tape.

We had tryouts for those who were to solo certain parts. One student said the first stanza as dramatically as possible, then the group cumulatively recited the same stanza immediately after. And, likewise, with different soloists for the second and third stanzas.

After the group's recitation of the entire poem, a student came forward and boasted that *they* certainly were not afraid of any lurpps. In fact, they would even sing about them to prove their courage. Thus, during presentations in the classrooms, the dramatists marched joyously around and through the students singing the poem. But as they finished, they quietly cupped their ears as some students exclaimed, "Oh, no, it's the lurpps!" This sent them, mockingly, squealing into flight. Whereupon, in came six monstrous-looking lurpps grabbing children left and right. Oh, the shrieks, looks of fright, and laughter! "Did you enjoy being scared?" I asked later. The response was a chorus of yesses.

Now that it is over how would I have rated our three presentations? The first one was a C+. We came back to the room and discussed what we liked and did not like about it. Next, for some unclear reason, we earned a D—and everyone knew it: Certain pupils had led the group incorrectly in the song, and they had had to start over; it was flat and not joyous in tone; and some of the solo and chorus parts were weak.

Apparently they did not want a repeat of that experience because on the third presentation they got an "A"—absolutely exciting and without a hitch. (Even my warming-up talk and conclusion with the class got a "You were pretty good, too, Mr. Charnock.") They were so buoyed by this experience that they requested to go into the fourth-grade class, which they had formerly not wanted to do because of the children's ages being so close to theirs and because of the nature or subject of the skit.

I have shared this experience with you because I wanted you to wade into the water with me. I have lots to learn, and am sure to have some attempts by my students and myself not work out, but we will never learn to swim if we give up because we swallow water once in a while.

Chapter 9

Diary Writing

I Hate It ...I Love It

If your students' experience with writing has been little or unpleasant, they may greet the idea of a daily activity of original, personal writing with much dislike. You may, in the beginning, have to be rather hard-nosed about it. It may take your stubbornness about two weeks to pay off because it may take some students that long to realize their initial attitude toward this kind of writing (or writing at all) is no longer justified.

In fact, within a month, you will most likely hear groans if you suggest that because of the need to cover some other curriculum area more thoroughly you are canceling diary writing for the day. Of course, this should never happen, but you might find it interesting to test the students' reactions.

A graphic example of this hate-then-love feeling toward diary writing is a recent fifth-grade class I visited. As soon as I mentioned the word "write" to the students there was a chorus of moans. Hands shot up like a forest of trees, and all the questions and statements were negative or laced with fear. Some said they were *not* going to write. Others that they didn't like writing. Would they have to correct their papers, they wanted to know. And on and on. After responding to several comments and questions, I announced that I would not answer any more questions, and, yes, everyone *would* write whether s/he wanted to or not. In other words, these students had such a dislike for writing that I could not persuade them of the enjoyment of personal writing. So, they would have to take diary writing much like medicine. Medicine isn't always pleasant to take, but it can cure you.

Well, the students, from all appearances, hated me, hated diary writing, and hated their teacher for asking me in.

Two weeks later I revisited the class to take a survey of the students' attitude toward diary writing, which the teacher had faithfully continued. They were told to be honest and their papers would be anonymous. They were asked to remember their feelings about diary writing on the first day and register their feelings about it then and their feelings about it now. Below are the results (translate numbers into percentages):

	Feelings	Before	After
1.	Terrible	21	7
2.	Bad	7	14
3.	Okay	57	14
4.	Good	7	7
5.	Very good	7	57

What is especially gratifying is that the "very good" category jumped from 7 percent to 57 percent. Had I thought to ask for the students' feelings on the first day of the diary writing, I am sure a greater percentage would have then selected numbers 1 and 2, making the change in interest even more dramatic. You should know, too, that the students hadn't yet experienced the possibility of voluntarily sharing with a chosen, close friend(s), which adds interest to the activity for some students.

What *Is* Diary Writing?

Diary writing, herein, is a form of sustained silent writing (SSW). Too briefly stated, SSW requires the student to fill up a period of time with writing. If the student cannot generate thought for original writing, then s/he can copy from any source or follow your prompting.

Additionally, SSW requires that you not grade the writing and, when SSW is diary writing, that you not read the writing at all without the student's request. (Diary writing could be called journal, or simply personal, writing for older students.)

Why Have Diary Writing?

First of all, personal writing does not, alone, satisfy the writing curriculum. Guided, structured writing—whether imaginative or practical—is just as necessary. By guided, structured writing is meant formal instruction in forming sentences, paragraphs, and larger compositions—including, for some examples, letters, reports, stories, and poems. This instruction, as with personal writing, should be related as much as possible to the experiences and interests of the students.

In contrast with formal instruction, personal writing does not limit the students' generation of ideas or hinder the natural flow of language. The students are simply responding to their reading, experiences, or fantasies. There is more of *them* in their writing and less of what others expect because their only audience is their future selves. On the other hand, if and when the time comes that they would like to share their written thoughts, they will most likely need to rewrite them to fit the new audience. This translation to please others is a much easier task for them now than if they had to do it initially.

Similar to other skills in life, writing is learned by writing. A daily routine fosters a habit. This is a major objective of SSW. For younger students, such daily writing also entails the struggling with phonetic-spelling patterns, a good reinforcer of lessons taught.

Personally, as well as academically, personal/diary writing helps the student think through ideas and feelings. It is comfortable, unpressured writing.

Your Diary-Writing Program: Some Ideas

1. Your students must be convinced that their personal writing will remain private. If a student wishes you to read the day's effort, s/he can place a marker in the booklet saying "Please read." You would then read the last entry and respond with a marginal comment.

2. Freedom to say what one wants is an important element in this activity. Students may, in fact, say they hate diary writing (only in the beginning, hopefully) or that they don't particularly like your teaching—then ask you to "Please read." Don't be offended—disarm them: To an I-hate-you comment, I once responded with, "I'm going to like you, anyhow. So there!" Or use a little humor: "You know down deep inside you have a secret liking for me!" (Well … nowadays, maybe not, but you get the idea.) The point is, some students will want to see if they are really free to write what they want. Apart from pure indecency, why not? Along this line, I would like to point out another value to diary writing. Most of the communication between teachers and students is one-way. We generate it; they passively receive it. Diary writing gives the students (if

they so desire) the opportunity to initiate written conversation with us; to share with us feelings, ideas, questions—for some people writing it is easier than saying it. I have been asked for advice about love, complimented on class activities, joked with, and—yes, it comes, too, if you are willing to be open to it—been unflatteringly criticized.

3. Each student should have his/her own writing booklet. It may be school-supplied or made by stapling lined sheets inside construction paper. Although the diary is the student's it should be collected at the end of each daily activity and locked away—it keeps temptation away from others. When the booklet is filled, the student may keep it.

4. You may wish to daily or frequently stimulate the flow of writing by providing a topic to write about (such as "Who Hates Me and Why") or an incomplete beginning sentence. Just prior to the writing period you might read the students a poem or short story to which they can respond. Or recall a school, local, or other incident for them to reflect upon. The students, of course, do not have to respond to your motivation techniques; they can write what they please, including copying from any source they wish. (Though you may wish to insist, from time to time, that the crutch of copying be abandoned for the day. Besides, they'll tire of such inane copying after a while.)

5. Silence should prevail so attention is not diverted from the task.

6. Students are to write continuously for a minimum of five (primary), ten (intermediate), or fifteen (junior

high) minutes. You may wish to write along with them or simply monitor them. But the students may well view diary writing as mere busy work if you engage in record keeping, paper-marking, tutoring and conversation with others. (Rather than a time requirement, some advocates of SSW stipulate that a certain *amount* be written—one-half to one page. This may not work for some students or teachers except at the end of the day when the teacher can keep the student to finish because students will produce at different rates and be finished at different times—creating a possible disciplinary-management problem. In addition, this approach makes writing feel like punishment.)

7. Additional motivation for some, on Fridays, can be to allow groups of three to assemble during diary writing to share their personal thoughts by reading a day's effort to the group and letting the group respond. Those who do not volunteer should be made comfortable about not doing so, but they must use this period in the usual way, by writing. Those sharing must do so quietly (otherwise, no sharing) and, if possible, be physically apart from the writers. (Some may find sharing contradictory to the idea of diary writing. But the student makes the decision to disclose, what to disclose, and to whom. Some students need the possibility of sharing to more thoroughly enjoy the other four days of writing. Certain students will never share their diaries and this is quite acceptable.)

8. Welcome and encourage students to share a writing effort with the entire class. (If you are writing, too, you may wish to set such an example.) Some diary-writing entries could be placed in a class or school

publication—with the permission of the author, of course. In the latter case, the piece might have to undergo personal editorial scrutiny by the student and teacher. The title for such a booklet might be "Secrets from Me to You" or "Our Secret Thoughts." Who could resist reading such a publication?!

9. Learning some capitalization, spelling, punctuation, and other requirements incidentally can take place without stifling the students' generation of ideas. You can insist that at the top of each entry the name of the week and month be correctly spelled and that the punctuation be properly placed. Capitalization in the title (each entry could be titled) and for the weekday and month should be required. Once the spellings of the weekdays and months have been learned, their correct abbreviations can be insisted upon along with the punctuation of the period. Even the insistence on margins (one-finger-wide) and the indentation of the first line will foster this habit for more formal writing.

10. One thing you will want to avoid is to take away diary writing for a disciplinary reason or to have it sporadically. If you are going to have it at all it should be daily and at the same time each day. Some find the end of the day best because the students can unwind and have a full school day of experiences from which to draw.

Some Diary Topics (Use Sparingly)

1. Who Hates Me and Why

2. Some Rotten Thoughts I've Had

3. I'll *Never* Tell You That …

4. How to Keep Your Girlfriend/Boyfriend

5. What People Think I'm Like, But What I'm Really Like

6. My Secret Crime

7. If I *Had* to Brag about Myself I'd Say This

8. What My Friends Disagree with Me About

9. Types of People I Can Do Without and Why

10. Me: the Good, the Bad

11. My Favorite Jokes

12. A Letter to Someone I Love

13. A Letter to Someone I Hate

14. My Spoiled Brother/Sister

15. The Time I Learned a Lesson

16. Some Things I Do That Are Babyish

17. Some Things I Do That Are Very Grown-up

18. The Fun of Being Sick

19. A Scary Dream I Had

20. When I Always Get Mad

21. Rainy Days

22. My Latest Dream

23. Why _____ Is the Best Sport to Watch/Play

24. A Good Teacher/Parent/Friend I know

25. Being the Only Child: Good Points; Bad Points

26. Being the Youngest/Oldest Child: Good Points; Bad Points

27. How I Help My Mother/Father

28. A Bad Habit I Know I Have

29. Why I Go to Church/Club

30. My Most Embarrassing Moment

31. How to Make School Better

32. My Classroom/Teacher: Likes, Dislikes

33. What Book Character I Am Most Like and Why

34. What Makes Teachers, Friends, and Others Like Me

35. What I'd Do If I Caught My Best Friend Doing Something Wrong

36. How I Spend My Weekends

37. Where I'd Go If I Had a Chance to Go Anywhere in the World

38. What I'd Like to Happen on My Birthday

39. How I "Catch" People on April Fools' Day

40. Some Reasons Students Use to Cut Class

41. Who I Admire Most

42. How I Feel about Having to Go to Bed Early on School Nights

43. How I Prepare to Give a Party

44. The Biggest Problem with Growing Up

45. Rich, Good-Looking, Athletic, or a Genius: Which I'd Rather Be If I Had to Choose One

46. How I Handle a Bad Report Card

47. What I'd Like to Change about Myself

48. Boys/Girls Have It Easier

49. The Biggest Mess I've Gotten Myself Into By Telling a Lie

50. The Luckiest Thing That Ever Happened to Me

51. I Hate_____—What Most Seem to Enjoy

52. I Like _____—What Most Seem to Hate

53. What, Me Worry? (Things I Worry About)

54. I May Be Broke, But I'll Always Find Money For …

55. I Accept Your Apology, Mom/Dad/Teacher/Friend

56. The Rules I Live By

57. If You Ask Me: My Opinion on a Number of Subjects

58. I'd Like to Protest: What Really Irks Me

59. My Most Terrible, Horrible, No Good, Very Bad Day

60. The History of an "Enemyship"/a Friendship

61. My Family: Both Serious and Silly

62. The Worst/Best Thing about Being A Teenager

63. Ways Girls/Boys Have It Easier/Harder

64. How I Deal with Conflicts with Girls/Boys

65. Continuing Experiences in My Life That Make Me Happy/Unhappy

66. The Story of My Life: A Mini-Novel

67. Peer Pressure: How It Affects Me

68. What I Would Like To Volunteer To Do

Chapter 10

Assisted Reading

When Students Aren't Learning Any Other Way

You are no doubt familiar with commercial and educational materials in which the text has been recorded and the student is to listen (and sometimes view) and "read" along. What often happens in such programs is that the student merely listens or watches and doesn't really concentrate on the reading.

"Assisted reading" is similar to this approach, but has the added factor of *requiring* the student to read along. Often a trade/library book is used, but the basal can also be recorded. The student is required to "read" (listen to) the short story or basal chapter (or chapter section) as many times as is necessary in order for her/him to read it independently to you or an aide (it is similar to "mastery learning"). The student is not allowed to read another listen-along book or go farther in the basal until the required assignment is 90-95 percent mastered. You can test the student by spot checking—selecting passages for the child to read aloud with fluency.

Basically, this is a sight-word approach, but phonetic patterns get picked up, too. It may seem boring, but some children who have not learned through the traditional phonics/word attack or traditional sight-word methods are able to see progress.

Most commercially recorded books (even if a video is used) are much too fast for this method. *You* have to record the story *slowly* (sometimes very slowly), but *expressively,* onto a tape, and be sure to mention the page number as you come to it. I have used this approach with some second and fifth graders and found it worked with those students who did *not* find it boring and had some drive or motivation to learn (which turned out to be about 50 percent of the participants [50 percent is better than zero]—how many others will be so frank?). Your experience may be better.

When library books are chosen, the tales should be short and have repetitive words and phrases as in *The Three Bears* or *Madeline* for younger readers. Students can be put on both trade and basal read-along programs. You might consider it better to skip parts of the basal if they are not interesting, but reality often dictates that it is the system by which the student's reading level is judged.

I give students the reward of one free paperback for each pair of trade books learned. (Paperbacks are much cheaper through book clubs that cater to schools.)

At first, with such poor readers, you or an aide may need to monitor closely. You may not wish to start all such students in the same library book or basal if you think competition will result—especially if those who move along the path to progress more slowly will socially suffer by their slowness. On the other hand, limited financial resources may force you to use the same book with all such students.

Students are allowed to use their finger to follow a line of print as the story is being read. Research and experience show that it may take about five listenings before the student can catch on to the procedure or is able to visually keep up even with a slowly-recorded piece of literature.

Some students will not profit or even like this method—even though they have not been learning otherwise. Other students will enjoy it and some will make dramatic progress. I had one fifth grader come to me reading at the PP level and within four months was ready for the 2.2 basal. (Unfortunately, he left my room and his next teacher was not interested in the approach regardless of how successful it was for him.)

Initially, assisted reading is a lot of work for you, so I can understand why most do not use it. There is also the expense of buying individual cassettes, and players for such, if the school budget cannot provide them. And the hours of recording the literature is more than some teachers are willing or able to commit to.

Just like other assignments, you can allow such students to take home these recordings you've made. Some students get hooked on this approach and want to make as much progress as they can. They will make more progress if they put more time into it—at home. In fact, if the student is self-conscious working in such a program among his/her peers, you may find it best that it be worked on only at home.

In conclusion, reading is not easy for some students and teaching such students is not easy for many teachers. Assisted reading *is* easy for both if both are willing to invest the needed time.

Reading Stories I've Finished

10.	
9.	
8.	
7.	
6.	
5.	
4.	
3.	
2.	
1.	

Name of Story

Your name: _____

Date started:_____   Date finished: _____

Chapter 11

Phonics and Syllables in the Middle and Upper Grades

Another Approach

Syllables are tied to phonics, and phonics are tied to … well, phonics, a rule-bound approach to learning and using sounds for written language.

The problem for middle-graders and above is that these rules have now become boring. My approach may not be thrilling, but it is surely simpler—like a computer shortcut that saves time. You might even call it rather silly, which I will take as a compliment.

A serious point is that middle and upper grade teachers just don't have the time to put the phonics-disadvantaged student (yes, I coined that phrase) through the slower process used in the primary grades. My approach is soundly philosophically-based; that is, it's *my* philosophy that older students can get from point A to point B in phonics more quickly *and* with some small amusement (and for the older student, phonics *is* small amusement).

Let's get down to business. Here are two truths: 1) Long vowel sounds (ai, a+e, and so on) appear easier to learn, and 2) short vowel sounds predominate in polysyllabic words. And "poly" is mostly the problem. For this reason, this method concentrates on the *short* vowel sounds—not only to help the student learn the sounds, but to help him or her decipher larger vocabulary. (More about this later in the "syllables" section.)

Phonics: Requirements, Prerequisites, Musts

This method *requires* each student who needs it to learn the short vowel sounds in the following way:

1. First, the student *must* memorize and say to you, in order (privately or in class), the following list of words: nat, net, nit, not, nut. (That's simple and silly enough.)

2. Then, s/he must be able to say: -at, -et, -it, -ot, -ut. (Some can say this immediately; therefore, they jump to step three.

3. Now, the student must "merely" say, in order, the short sound of each vowel: a, e, i, o, u. (Note that e and i are often sounded alike by the students—or one is omitted. Be strict on both of these being distinctly sounded—unless there is a speech or hearing problem.)

4. Finally, the student must listen to *you* say the short vowel sounds *out of order*. The student must get them all correct, several times. Plus, you must ask the *student* to make the sounds out of order several times. Only then has the student passed the Charnock Phonics Test, but there is no law against reinforcement.

Syllabication Made Simple

If you haven't realized it already, many of the "officially sanctioned" rules for syllable division are not just onerous to learn, but of little practical value. Yes, our vanity forces us to consult a dictionary if we want to know the "accepted" splitting of a word, but even Mr. Webster's syllables count for very little when it comes to correctly talking, reading, or writing a word. This may sound akin to pedagogical heresy, but just keep on reading. (You do know that most word processors or computers can be set to eliminate word-dividing altogether.)

Another wild idea is that "syllable knowledge," itself, isn't that important and therefore, unless it *must* be taught in your school, you should pay it little attention. But since you probably don't have that luxury—or being a maverick doesn't suit your fancy—let's make this as painless as possible.

The Mr. Charnock rule that, for the most part, one can pronounce *every* vowel as short in polysyllabic words, helps, but one needs to know the short sounds. What this really amounts to is the student using common sense and seeing little words or familiar combinations within larger words. If you think your students' attention needs to be focused on *this* idea, read on.

Rules: You Can't Get Away from Them

Most vowels in polysyllabic words are short. (Trust me on this.) And if only a minority are long, so what? Let the student pronounce the syllable's vowel sound short; if it happens to be long, and the word is in her or his oral/aural vocabulary, the student will correct it. If the student doesn't have the word in his or her vocabulary bank or doesn't correct the pronunciation, does it really matter? Not much.

Before you begin to formally teach syllables, students should understand the basics of phonics. That is, they should know the consonant, blend, digraph, and vowel sounds, and be aware that there is one vowel sound per syllable. They should, also, be familiar with the ideas of root word, prefix, and suffix.

After the students know the above basics, teach them only *five* strategies for dividing words into syllables: *Always* try to divide a word into a CV-CV (consonant-vowel) pattern as follows:

1. (al-li-ga-tor)—*unless overruled* by one of the three remaining strategies.

2. Divide the word between two consonants (sil-ver).

3. Divide the word after a prefix (re-make).

4. Divide the word before a suffix (hate-ful).

5. Don't divide blends of any kind (including digraphs) or leave dangling consonants.

Remember that students are always allowed to use short vowel sounds for words of three or more syllables. Also, be sure to point out that sentence context and familiar patterns within words give lots of pronunciation clues.

I'm sure your students will find the Charnock Method of syllabication simpler to understand and easier to acquire. (Throw out that archaic "opened" and "closed" syllable language.) Your students will be able to pronounce the most fantastically long words they'll meet, and that's what syllabication is supposed to be good for, anyhow—whether it comes naturally or has to be taught.

More Help

Some people want as concrete as possible an explanation to fully understand a concept (I'm one of those). So, the following chart is my attempt at being eruditely clear on the Charnock Method of syllabication:

Polysyllabic Proficiency[1]

I. Probable Prerequisite Knowledge
  A. Consonants: single (t), blended (tr, nd), digraphic (th)
  B. Vowels: short (a as in cat), long (ea, a+e, final y), blended (oil), r-controlled (ir)
  C. One vowel sound per syllable (except -ple, -ble, and so on)— and no single consonant
  D. Common prefixes, suffixes (root word knowledge)
II. Sensible Strategies to Use

(A)	(B)	(C)	(D)[2]
C-C	Prefix-	-Suffix	CV-CV
sil-ver	re-make	hate-ful	al-li-ga-tor

III. Petty Problems[3]

st-rain	re-ign	whisper-ed	vi-o-lin[4]
fas-t		raking[5]	(a-ve-rage
		objec-tion-a-ble	a-ver-age
			av-er-age)[6]

Explanation

1. Grades 4 and up—although primary teachers will find some of this information useful, too.

2. Student always tries to get the CV-CV pattern *unless* overruled by rules II,A,B,C. Student allowed to use short vowel sound for all audible single vowels in words of three or more syllables (not: a-ble,-ate, -y). (Of course, this does not mean you abandon the teaching of spelling /spelling patterns.)

3. Sentence context and familiar combinations in words give lots of pronunciation clues.

4. The "io" is not a learned vowel blend or digraph pattern; therefore, it can be considered divisible.

5. Mistakenly pronounced as "rakking."

6. Demonstrates sometimes-practical limitation of a polysyllabic division rules in words of three or more syllables. Either division of this example has little effect on pronunciation or understanding.

Chapter 12

Killing *Three* Birds with One Stone

or

Using Picture Books to Improve the Mechanics of Public Speaking and Overcome Stage Fright in Middle, Junior, and High School Students; Inform Primary Grade Teachers of Good Literature; and Interest Young Listeners in Reading

(If your school does not have primary grades, but is a middle, junior, or even high school, the following program will also work for you if there is a primary school nearby. Simply make arrangements as per this chapter; what better way to have interscholastic cooperation!)

For two or three months every year my students (any grade from five through eight) visit our kindergartens and primary grades to read picture books to them. The student self-selects a book from among those I have provided, silently reads through it several times, orally practices with one or two fellow students and sometimes at home with a parent—all in the span of a week.

The next preparatory effort is the scariest. Even though the student has an idea what s/he is getting into, s/he has no idea what s/he's getting into. Each student must stand in front of the class and demonstrate effective techniques in using the book. I'm looking for, and demanding: clarity, expression, good eye contact with the audience, modulated voice volume, varied reading speeds, and a sense of poise. I also expect the student to master holding the book so the pictures can be seen by the class during reading. And, right off, I don't tolerate a poor attitude or ridicule from the class.

As you can well expect, very few students pass this test first time up. Some need to repeat their public reading up to six times. They are frightened and I am sympathetic, empathetic … and firm. But to ease them into this program, I demonstrate by reading several picture books to the class during the week they are practicing on their own. And when a student does stand in front of the class and is not adequate in presentation, I interrupt, take the book and show the student and class how it could be presented. I give helpful criticism and sometimes allow the class to do so also—respectfully.

This activity is not voluntary. At least 50 percent of the student's speech grade for the period will be based on the cooperating teacher's evaluation of the student's performance.

Although a majority of my students eagerly participate, at first, a few state a strong dislike for the assignment, vow they will *not* perform in this fashion, feign a headache on the day of their debut before their primary class, or think up some other ingenious way to get out of the assignment: stomach ache, sore throat … you name it. (It doesn't work.) A few give a plain admission of overwhelming fear. For two or three students—out of a class of thirty—I may have to actually *insist* they report to the cooperating teacher. (This fear is so strong the principal often reports, early on, seeing isolated students cowering at a teacher's door, afraid to return to my class but also fearful of taking that bold step across the threshold into a frightening situation.)

Then something almost miraculous happens. After the first or second public reading, it is amazing to witness the student who was so panic-stricken to now practically insist on going more often. There is just something about "being on stage"— especially when the audience gives rapt attention and claps when you are finished (and when you are well prepared).

The student sticks with the one chosen book throughout the program, but reads it to six or seven classes. And with each additional class performance becomes more relaxed, more confident in his/her skill, more dramatic, and experiences the good feeling of being successful.

As stated in the long subtitle, the purposes for this program are: 1) to help the participating student improve in the mechanics of public speaking and overcome some stage fright, 2) to share with the cooperating teacher a variety of picture books and help provide a possible springboard for a literature lesson, and 3) to interest the student being read to in some possibly-unknown library/trade book selections. This chapter is really about number one, but the latter two take effect simultaneously. Teachers frequently express delight in hearing a story of which they are unaware (I keep searching for suitable books) and sometimes use the book (even my student) in helping their pupils creatively respond to the story. Teachers also report that the school librarian is deluged with requests from the children for the books they have heard.

This past year I thought the cooperating teachers would like to know how my students felt about the program they helped make possible. I took a survey of answers to two questions about the program. We used the rating of 1 through 5, 1 meaning "very little" and 5 meaning "very much." Here are the results:

1. Did you enjoy the experience, on average?

   59 percent rated the experience as a 5

   88 percent rated the experience as either a 4 or 5

2. Did storyreading help you overcome some performance shyness?

   59 percent rated the help as a 5

   83 percent rated the help as either a 4 or 5

I asked the participants to voluntarily relate their personal feelings about their storyreading experience. There were no negative comments, and following are several positive ones:

Hung: It helped my performance attitude and voice expression.

Renee: When I first went down to read I was kind of scared, but the second and third time I felt like "nothing can stop me now." I felt like I could keep on reading to classes forever.

Elaine: At first I was scared, but now I have fun reading because now I know what it means to the children when I read to them.

Adrian: My performance in front of little students has really improved. I feel as though I can read in front of any little kid in the world and won't be scared. It has helped me give better speeches to my class upstairs. I think I just took my first giant step: overcoming fear.

Khadijah: When I went down to read to the children downstairs I was real scared. But when I got down there, the teachers talked to me to try and make me loosen up and stop acting shy. After I went a few times it was easy.

Maysee: When I first went down, I was very scared that I would not do well, but the kids and teachers were very nice and I really enjoyed it. Most of all I liked it a lot because it gave me a chance to prove to myself that I can do anything as well as others.

Christine: My experience was really great! I liked reading in front of the classes and watching the children's reactions to what I read. If I could I would do it all over again.

As you may gather from the above comments—especially Adrian's—this program also served as a technique to ease the students into the more frightening task of public speaking; such as giving a report on a book or research project. This program uses a crutch, the picture book, but it is good training for non-crutch performance.

**STUDENT STORYREADING
EVALUATION SHEET**

Student_____

Book_____

(Rating System: 1=needs improvement, 2=passing, 3=good, 4=very good)

Speech clarity _____	Self confidence (poise)_____
Voice expression _____	Voice volume _____
Facial expression _____	Reading speed _____
Holding book _____	General attitude _____

Teacher _____ Room _____

Date _____

(Using the rating scale, the numbers 1 through 4 equaled the letters E through B in the area of public speaking. No A was given because the student was not truly speaking as when giving a report—of course, you may wish to devise your own rating scale. Nevertheless, an A could be earned in other ways.)

There were many good picture books we could not use. Usually those that could be read in five to ten-plus minutes and had large, clear illustrations that could be appreciated from the back of the classroom were the most successful for this whole-class approach. (I found teachers more amenable to having my students read to the whole class than to a small group since the former method was easier to schedule and less disruptive to the teacher's program.)

Most of the following books easily satisfy the requirement of a short text with large illustrations. Some will be shelved with picture books and some with folk tales. The list is rather long because you will not find all of them in your school or public library (though none are of very recent publication), and because your students may not like certain ones—such preferences must be allowed. After each book is a suggested listener interest range.

Aardema, Verna. *Oh, Kojo! How Could You!* (1-3)
Allard, Harry. *Miss Nelson Is Missing* (K-3)
    Miss Nelson Has a Field Day (K-3)
Arkin, Alan. *Tony's Hard Work Day* (1-2)
Bemelmans, Ludwig. *Madeline* (K-2)
Bishop, Claire. *The Five Chinese Brothers* (K-2)
Blume, Judy. *The Pain and the Great One* (K-3)
Briggs, Raymond. *Jim and the Beanstalk* (K-3)
Brown, Kay. *Jack and the Beanstalk* (K-3)
Brown, Marc. *Arthur's Eyes* (K-3)
    Arthur's Tooth (K-3)
    Arthur's Valentine (K-3)
Brown, Marcia. *The Neighbors* (K-3)
Calhoun, Mary. *The Hungry Leprechaun* (1-3)
Carlson, Bernice. *We Want Sunshine in Our Houses* (1-3)
Carrick, Carol. *A Clearing in the Forest* (K-3)
Carrick, Carol & Donald. *A Clearing in the Forest* (1-3)

Cauley, Lorinda. *Three Little Pigs* (K-2)
Crowe, Robert. *Clyde Monster* (K-3)
Crowley, Arthur. *The Boogey Man* (1-3)
Domanska, James. *Why So Much Noise?* (1-3)
Freeman, Don. *Corduroy* (K-2)
Galdone, Paul. *The Amazing Pig* (K-3)
    Cinderella (1-3)
    The Elves and the Shoemaker (1-3)
    The Gingerbread Boy (K-3)
    Little Red Hen (K-1)
    Little Red Riding Hood (K-2)
    The Monkey and the Crocodile (K-3)
    The Monster and the Tailor (K-3)
    Obedient Jack (K-3)
    The Princess and the Pea (1-3)
    Rumpelstiltskin (1-3)
    Tailypo (1-3)
    The Three Bears (K-1)
    The Three Billy Goats Gruff (K-2)
    The Three Sillies (1-3)
    The Three Wishes (K-3)
    The Turtle and the Monkey (K-3)
    What's in Fox's Sack? (K-3)
Grabianski, Janusz. *Androcles and the Lion* (1-3)
Griffith, Helen V. *Plunk's Dreams* (K-3)
Grindley, Sally. *I Don't Want To!* (K-3)
Gurney, Nancy & Eve. *The King, the Mice and the Cheese* (K-3)
Hoban, Russel. *Harvey's Hideout* (K-3)
Hoff, Sid. *Lengthy* (K-2)
Hoffman, Mary. *Amazing Grace* (1-3)
Hogrogian, Nonny. *One Fine Day* (K-2)
Houston, John. *A Mouse in My House* (1-3)
Ipcar, Dahlov. *The Cat Came Back* (K-3)
Kahl, Virginia. *The Perfect Pancake* (2-3)
Kent, Jack. *Clotilda* (K-2/3)
    The Fat Cat (K-3)
    Joey Runs Away (K-3)

There's No Such Thing As a Dragon (1-3)
   Silly Goose (K-3)
Kimishima, Hisako. *Ma Lien and the Magic Brush* (1-3)
Kraus, Robert. *Another Mouse to Feed* (1-3)
Levintin, Sonia. *Nobody Stole the Pie* (K-3)
Lobel, Arnold. *Giant John* (K-3)
   Ming Lo Moves the Mountain (1-3)
McCloskey, Robert. *The Man Who Lost His Head* (1-3)
McGovern, Ann. *Too Much Noise* (K-2)
Mayer, Mercer. *What Do You Do with a Kangaroo?* (K-3)
Mosel, Arlene. *Tikki, Tikki, Tembo* (1-3)
Peet, Bill. *Eli* (1-3)
Pinkwater, Daniel. *I Was a Second Grade Werewolf* (1-3)
Polushkin, Maria. *The Little Hen and the Giant* (k-3)
Prelutsky, Jack. *The Mean Old Mean Hyena* (K-3)
Schlatz, Letta. *The Extraordinary Tug of War* (K-2)
Dr. Seuss. *I Had Trouble in Getting to Solla Sollew* (1-3)
   Thidwick the Big-Hearted Moose (1-3)
Steig, William. *Sylvester and the Magic Pebble* (1-3)
Stevens, Janet. *Androcles and the Lion* (K-3)
Tripp, Wallace. *The Tale of a Pig* (1-2)
Ungerer, Tomi. *Strega Nona* (1-3)
   Zeralda's Ogre (K-3)
Waber, Bernard. *Ira Sleeps Over* (1-3)
Whitney, Alma. *Just Awful* (K-3)
   Leave Herbert Alone (K-2)
Williams, Barbara. *Albert's Toothache* (K-3)
Wiseman, B. *Don't Make Fun* (K-3)
Zemach, Harve. *The Judge* (2-3)
Zemach, Margot. *It Could Always Be Worse* (1-3)
Zion, Gene. *Harry the Dirty Dog* (K-2)

STORYREADING PROGRAM WEEK OF _____

DAY	TIME	TEACHER	RM	GRADE	STORY READER

Note to the teacher: Fill in after consulting teachers. Change weekly. To make this chart more eye appealing, write/print the title in bold red and the column headings in bold blue. You may wish to enlarge via photocopying.

Chapter 13

How to Gain a Reputation

How many times have you been confronted by one of your students with the statement, "Tell me a good library book so I can get it"? And you couldn't get your mind in gear before the student decided to abandon you, in your embarrassment, and began to meander aimlessly through the bookshelves.

Or maybe you *were* quick-thinking enough to remember a book of interest, but felt at a loss for words that would grab the student's interest.

Even then you may have found yourself rattling off too much of the story, or, on the other hand, overemphasizing what a *great* book it is, a *really* great book, because that is all you could remember.

The truth of the matter is most of us do not read enough children's and young adults' books. In fact, if students ask us, on a regular basis, to recommend a good book, that makes us rare: We have been attributed with the reputation for knowing what is good to read.

Not all of us lack this reputation through any great fault of our own. Our day is crowded at school and away with demands beyond the average. Our job, though often rewarding, is an exhausting one. And there is never enough time or energy to accomplish all we would like to as teachers, especially experiencing enough books to recommend or read aloud to our class(es).

Nevertheless, not possessing *some* reputation for knowing good books is the fault of some teachers. We know those who never read to their students and who, presumably, never know of any books beyond their own childhood favorites to recommend—should they be asked, which they most likely won't be. Then, there are those who have become familiar with enough books to fill up a year's worth of daily (or, alas, weekly) story time, a fifteen- to twenty-minute event. These last teachers can be more professionally admired, but even they lack—and would most likely admit it—the resourceful knowledge needed to help turn their students into avid and wide readers.

The more we realize the responsibility for instilling a *love* of reading in students, the more we will feel the need to become familiar with many and different types of books with which to entice them.

Once we desire to increase our familiarity with many more books, there are two approaches we can take. The first is simply to supply the students with a list of recommended books (better yet, to round up a few books on the list). Or we can become personally acquainted with a lot more children's and/or young adults' books. The latter course will give the greatest pleasure and make us more professionally competent in this area. It will also add to our reputation as a person who knows a lot of good books to read. And as teachers of reading (and here I include content area teachers, too) we *should* have such a personal knowledge and reputation.

What does the foregoing mean for you? A lot of work. But nothing so good as what you can become can be easily gotten. It will require many hours of reading before you will have a respectable beginning knowledge that can be relied upon to aid your desire to foster a greater hunger for reading. Your first goal should be to have a resource of at least 100 books you like. Note that I did not say to read: You may have to read 150 or more to get the 100 you appreciate. But 100 is the bare minimum. Two hundred would be a better beginning goal. And even with 200 books of different genres and varying degrees of difficulty, you will find the need to become even more knowledgeable. Your need will never stop.

Choosing books you can recommend or read aloud is quite a simple matter. If a book bores you, you can assume it may affect your students likewise—of course, we know that's not always true. If it is a slow starter, are your students mature enough to hang in there until it gets more interesting later? (Don't dismiss all books on this account, however, because some students can handle such books.) Does the story encourage humor or compassion? Does it foster imagination or fascination? Remember, if you like the book, it is likely to be a winner for you (as a read-aloud) and your students.

But here's the surprise: Once you favorably decide on a book, your job isn't over. There is no way you will be able to adequately articulate your fascination with the book when it eventually becomes number three in a quantity of a hundred or more. So you should sit right down and get in touch with your feelings immediately upon finishing reading and write what you feel. Remember, your objective is to interest your students: Advertise the book and direct the ad to them in a style they will enjoy. (A warning: Once finished reading a book, if you lay it aside because you don't presently have the time to write an ad for it, you may never get that intense feeling back.)

"Wait a minute!" I can hear some of you protesting. "What's wrong with letting the kid read the book's cover flap or the blurbs on the back?" My answer is that when one peruses such writings with the intended juvenile reader in mind the answer becomes clear. The overviews and quotes on a book's cover are too frequently not much help in creating an interest within the intended consumer. Too often the message is inadequately brief (which can also be said of juvenile book club blurbs), heavily (analytically) written, or seems to be addressing adults. And such writing is seldom provocative enough to use in *introducing* the book. Or, on the other hand, it might be quite deceptive: We have all read exciting ads for dull books. Of course, when the writing is superb and accurate it should be used. Most importantly of all, relying upon the book cover to advertise a book simply gives one another excuse not to become personally acquainted with the contents of many books for children.

Now that you are convinced, I hope, what you need next is "The Book Ads File." This will become an indispensable aid to student library visits, to SSR periods, and as a story time or book-introducing resource for you. Some students will also enjoy writing ads for the books they have read. Simply include them in the file.

Just how broad your ad collection will be depends on your interest and your perception of the need to widen your students' reading fare. I suggest various genres be included (science fiction, fantasy, realistic fiction, biography, for examples), issues (death, drug use, dating, slavery, divorce, war, etc.), and informational books. A primary grade teacher will have a greater number of picture-book ads than the intermediate and junior high teacher, who will probably have more realistic fiction ads.

On the back of each book-ad card could be recorded the book's theme(s) and ways the students can be helped to engage with the book as a class—often referred to as "responding to literature."

Finally, to give a concrete idea of what I am writing about, here are some ads I have composed for a range of grades. I wrote them on 4-inch by 6-inch cards, laminated them, and filed them by literature category, but others may wish to organize their ads differently. I often gather up a few of the books written about and hold them up to the class as I "advertise" them, reading the ads. You should see the hands shoot up!

ARE YOU THERE GOD? IT'S ME, MARGARET

By Judy Blume
(Dell paperback, 149 pages)

She was still flat … so she put cotton balls in her bra (why not?); she was about twelve, but would she be the last of her friends to have her period? She wasn't any religion, but that didn't keep her from talking to God—even if she was upset with Him sometimes. Read about friendships, enemyships, and "girl problems," about Margaret Simon, but you'll probably see yourself, too.
(Realistic Fiction)

CHERNOWITZ!

By Fran Arrick
(Bradbury Press, 165 pages)

"Cherno" isn't good enough. If you're Jewish, you've got to sound it. Not Cherno—Chernowitz. Like Horowitz. That way everybody knows you're a "Jew bastard" and "Christ killer." Who feels this way? Emmett Sundback, a ninth-grade bully. Not too bright in most ways, but he's sure got it right—so he feels—about Jews.

Every day Bobby Cherno dreads going to school. Not only does he have to face the sneering comments of Emmett, but also his "gang"—students who used to be Bobby's friends.

Finally, after over a year of torture, Bobby decides to fight back dirty—just like Emmett. He's going to get revenge.

A powerful story.
(Realistic Fiction)

MISS NELSON IS MISSING

By Harry Allard & James Marshall
(Houghton Mifflin, 30 pages)

"Keep your mouths shut!" said Miss Swamp.
"Keep perfectly still!" said Miss Swamp.
"And if you misbehave, you'll be sorry!" said Miss Swamp.
Well, the kids in Room 207 are the worst-behaving class in the whole school and now they've got just what they deserve: Miss Viola Swamp, a substitute and a real witch as far as the kids are concerned.

And what happened to sweet Miss Nelson, their regular teacher? The kids become so overworked, underloved, and just plain miserable that they go hunting for her. But they can't find her. Is she missing? Not really. Is she hiding? Sort of. Just where will surprise you.

A fun book to read.
(Picture Book: Fanciful Humor)

THUMBS UP, THUMBS DOWN
STUDENT-RATED BOOKS

BOOK TITLE	1	2	3	4	5	STUDENT RATER

RATINGS: (1) Too uninteresting to finish; (2) Finished, but it wasn't that great; (3) Better than most—at least *I* liked it; (5) So good I think anyone would like it. (Just place a check mark in the box.)

To the teacher: To add eye appeal, make the title in bold red, subtitle in bold blue, and column headings in bold black.

Chapter 14

A Mini-Potpourri of Ideas to Spark Structured Creativity

Too many teachers limit their compositional writing instruction to what is called "creative" or "imaginative"—as though neither could apply to more practical efforts. Then they try to balance this over-emphasis by lots of grammar work and red-penciling.

Most of this volume deals with the structure of writing, but this chapter lets you dabble in a few other approaches that, admittedly, border on the creative. But, still, you must lead the student by example, i.e., use a page herein for instruction or, better yet, devise your own examples. Later, use your best students' best writings and other activities (with their permission) as examples when you revisit these formats next week or next year.

The Creative Use of One Word

"The Down Story"

By K.T.

I went downtown yesterday to watch football. Players were being knocked <u>down</u> and some fell <u>down</u>. As the game progressed players were either worn <u>down</u> or broke <u>down</u> in tears.

Then the next morning when I walked into the classroom on the first day of school, students were having a nervous break-<u>down</u>. As the day went on, the teacher had to settle <u>down</u> the class. When it got noisier he made us walk up and <u>down</u> the stairs.

At the end of the day, when everyone stepped outside into the snowy, cold day, people had to put on their <u>down</u>-lined coats.

And whoever reads this story will probably be worn <u>down</u> from reading all the <u>down</u> words.

Writing Creative Ads

Assignment

Advertise anything not usually advertised on TV, radio or in print. Or choose something that is often advertised, but not used in the way *you* have chosen. You will want to give your reader one or more reasons for buying your product. Try to make your reader want, even feel, that she or he *needs,* your creation. Some ideas: If you need a little help, here are just a few. But you can make up any product or product use you wish.

One bottle is all you will ever need to purchase!

Examples:

*shoe laces

*candy shoe laces

*doggie paw warmer

Finally, draw a picture and color it.

Gargle-2

How many times have you spit good money down the drain? If you use Scope, Lavoris or Listermint, that's exactly what you do!

But NEW, SCIENTIFICALLY FOR-MULATED **Gargle-2** can be reused. Don't spit it into the sink after one use; put it-slobber and all-back into the CONVE-NIENT, FLIP-TOP bottle of **Gargle-2**.

The bacteria-fighting agents in **Gargle-2** will kill all the germs that came out of your mouth. And when the contents of of your mouth washing is added to the yet unused portion of **Gargle-2**, it will be re-strengthened to fight bad breath once more.

So, have a clean-smelling breath and SAVE MONEY, too!

Gargle-2—at all good stores every-where.

Writing Realistic Ads

Use the following real estate ad as an example to write a similar ad for your house. Walk around the house, room by room, floor by floor. Then talk to your parents. Get all the positives you can—without being too wordy—to sell your house. Be creative, but don't exaggerate. Take a picture of the inside or out to display.

INTRODUCING 604 Carson Run
Road, Upper Darby, PA 19082

A picture of your house
goes here.

Price: $120,000 (built 1940)
Style: Brick exteriored townhouse
Heating System: Gas hot air
Hot Water: Gas. Tank age: 8 years
Roof: 15 years
Electrical Service: 120 & 200 amps
Taxes: $2,000, approximately
Lot Size: 18 x 94 ft.
School System: Upper Darby

1st Floor: Here is a spacious and attractive living-dining area and a partially-opened kitchen. The latter is modern with ample cabinetry and the convenience of a dishwasher. For summer pleasure there is a front patio. And, especially if you have small children or a pet, there is the fenced yard. To keep the cold and wet out of the house, there is the ever-practical vestibule. This house is cable-TV ready.

2nd Floor: Here are a master bedroom with a walk-in closet, middle and smaller bedrooms with sizable closets, a modern ceramic tiled bath, and a hall linen closet.

Basement: A clean, tiled, unfinished basement with a utility area and integral garage that you may want to make a walk-in one day.

Remarks

This is one of the newer and nicest blocks in the area. And superior to many of the other houses are the three bedrooms instead of two AND a garage. Seldom will you see such ample and modern kitchen cabinets—even in a larger kitchen. The openness between the living and dining areas and partial openness to the kitchen adds a sense of spaciousness that few townhouses offer.

You will be ideally located for transportation and shopping. And, this being a townhouse, your heating and cooling expenses will be less. Most windows have been replaced with efficient, easy-to-clean storms—only five years old, including the storm doors. The plush carpets are only three years old.

Offer includes: all air conditioners, refrigerator, washer, dryer, and dishwasher.

This *Is* Writing

No, this is not art. And, yes, it is basic to writing. This is a tool to orally teach giving, following, and writing directions. More importantly, it teaches language precision, that is, *saying* exactly what one means. Which, hopefully, transfers to *writing* exactly what one means. Clarity and conciseness does not come easily to young writers or the rest of us. This is a fun activity that students never seem to tire of.

Here's how you do it. Duplicate each of the following drawings (you can make your own, too [maybe something more familiar]; these were "drawn" with the computer) onto a 12-by-18-inch oaktag sheet. (Double the sheet so light won't show through.) Have one volunteer go to the board. Show the drawing to the class behind the student's back—who is not allowed to turn around, but just listen and draw with chalk. Classroom audience volunteers, one at a time, tell the student how to draw the object with no hint as to what it is—or any part of it. The "instructors" are not allowed to use their hands to clarify their directions. They must use language like, "Draw a straight horizontal line midway on the blackboard for about as long as your forearm." And thus they will continue. All along, you are holding the drawing up for the class to see how precise the instructions are being given. When there are too many mistakes, another audience member needs to be chosen.

The person at the board doesn't get off scot-free, either. If, after a while, that person can't pick up on when correct, precise language is given, a replacement is needed—which means, of course, a couple of students will need to be waiting in the hall so they will not see the drawing in advance. Students can also play this game in small groups.

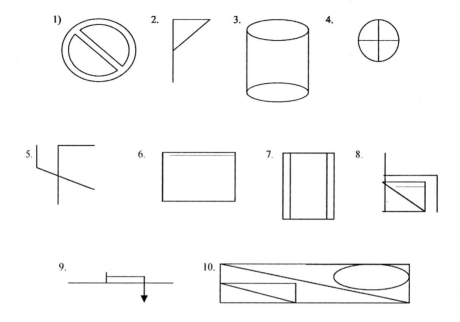

Featuring a Family

Your school—Your street—Your town

Dear Parents:

How would you like to be in the movies? On TV? On a classroom or hallway bulletin board? Well, we can't promise the former two, but the latter one is definitely possible.

Our class would like to feature its families. (Which is also a way of making each participating student a star for a period of time.) We believe the family to be very important in a student's school progress, and would like to put them in the limelight. If you would like to participate in this fun activity, here are two suggestions that will prove interesting to the class and others:

1. Send clear pictures of your family (both individual and group, if possible) including all members of the household: grandparents, aunts, uncles, even pets.

2. A shot of adults on-the-job and on-the-hobby would be of interest.

3. Be aware that we will laminate these with captions on posterboard—so you might want to send copies rather than the originals.

If you can provide us with as much of the following information as possible (or as much as you wish) about each member, we can arrange an interesting display. All blanks on the accompanying form may not apply to every member. Please use this number format on additional sheets of paper for each pictured member (or make photocopies).

Sincerely,
Your Name
Teacher

FEATURE-FAMILY FORM

1. Student's name: _____

2. Your name: _____

3. Relation to student: _____

4. Job description: _____

_____

_____

5. Other jobs held (previous & now): _____

_____

_____

6. Hobby, special skill/talent: _____

_____

7. Distant travel: _____

_____

8. Awards/honors: _____

_____

_____

9. If a graduate of this school, please check here: _____

Chapter 15

Fun with Vocabulary

You will find sacrosanct word lists galore from workbook, textbook, and e-book publishers. The truth is that there is no such creature as sacrosanct vocabulary when it comes to teaching, the Miller Analogies Test aside. It makes sense to include phonetically oriented words for the learner of reading and subject-matter words for students to understand and spell, but beyond that students pick up words via a rich source of reading and study. So, if you want your students to develop a good vocabulary, interest them in varied reading—and its partner, writing.

At the junior high level I never had spelling tests, but vocabulary exams: words that were taken from our study. And to make it fun, I always included humorous words that are still in use today (a list will follow).

If you really want the student to know a word, incidentally or directly introduce it beforehand. And when Friday comes, the exam is quite different from most spelling tests. I give the first letter of the word, announce the number of syllables, give the meaning, and omit it from an oral sentence. If the student has studied, s/he will recall the word. This might seem like giving the student too much help, but the objective is more to get the student to know and use (and they do) the word rather than to test his or her memory. Most of my junior high students (though I would start in the fifth grade) thoroughly enjoyed my including and using "funny-sounding" words.

Here is a list of informative words you can weave into your usually mandatory spelling or vocabulary curriculum:

adieu: Goodbye, farewell (French)

afoot: On foot, walking (There is mischief afoot.)

balderdash: Nonsense

bamboozle: Trick someone for evil purposes and hiding true intentions

bedazzle: To impress greatly (and usually positively)

bigwig: VIP

birdbrain: Stupid, foolish person (a scatterbrain)

brouhaha: Uproar, hubbub, commotion

buffaloed: Baffled, bewildered; sometimes with a sense of outsmarting

buffoon: Always clowning or tying to be funny, but laughed at more than with

city slicker: Rural slang (opposite of country bumpkin) for a well-dressed, educated city dweller (especially one visiting a rural area)

cootie: Parasitic insect: lice, etc.

dawdle: To waste time, saunter when walking or engaging in a pursuit

debut: First public appearance

diddlysquat: Of little or no value (Slang: That doesn't mean diddlysquat)

dilly dally: Waste time by loitering

din: Loud, continuous noise

ding-a-ling: Stupid, foolish, eccentric person

dolt: Stupid, slow-witted person; blockhead

dun: Repeated, insistent demand for payment

fiddle-faddle: Nonsense, trivial (n.)

flabbergasted: Shocked with surprise or wonder

flimflam: Fraud (tricking to get money)

flip-flop: Unexpected, sudden reversal of belief, policy (many similar meanings)

flippant: Shallow, disrespectful remark about what many hold as dear

fuddy-duddy: Old-fashioned, pompous, critical, concerned about trifles

gewgaw: Uselessly showy article of wear (trinket, bauble)

gobbledygook: Roundabout (purposely confusing?) way to communicate

greenhorn: Inexperienced in task or local customs

harebrained: Dimwitted, scatterbrained

helter-skelter: Disorderly haste, haphazard manner, carelessly hurried

highfalutin: better-than-you-are attitude

hobnob: To socially associate

hocus-pocus: To confuse, play a trick on via cloaking the truth (deception)

hodge-podge: Jumbled assembly (miscellany)

hogwash: Worthless, meaningless talk or writing (bunk)

hokum/bunkum: Pretentious nonsense

hoodwink: To deceive or trick (dupe, cheat, swindle, gyp)

hooey: Nonsense

hootenanny: Folksong festival where the audience often joins in

horn swoggle: To swindle, cheat, hoodwink

horsefeathers: Not worth considering, rubbish—expresses contempt

hotsy-totsy: Fine, splendid, perfect

hubbub: Noise by people over what some consider insignificant

humbug: Nonsense (various meanings)

humdinger: Usually preceded by "a real ..."; extraordinary person or thing

hunky-dory: Everything is fine

hurly-burly: Noisy disorder or commotion

ilk: Kind, sort, class; usually preceded by "of that …"

imp: Devilish, mischievous child (usually said with fondness)

ire: Anger, wrath

irk: Annoy, irritate (also irksome)

itsy-bitsy: Very small

jimjams: The jitters; extremely nervous

kowtow: To not dare cross, but be servant-like to another (a bully, boss, law)

lickety-split: At great speed

local yokel: Native and gullible inhabitant of rural area/small town

mealy mouthed: Not willing to state the facts in simple, direct words; insincere

meander: A winding, indirect way of reaching a goal

moxie: Courage

muckraker: One who searches for and exposes "dirt" or scandal on another

mumbo jumbo: Language used to confuse; meaningless language

namby-pamBy Lacking in character, weak, indecisive

nincompoop: Fool, simpleton

nitty-gritty: The basics

nitwit: Scatterbrain

numbskull: dull-witted, stupid person

obnoxious: highly offensive; disgustingly objectionable; repugnant

okeydokey: Agreement. Sometimes "Okeydoke."

old coot: Foolish, stupid senile and unpleasant person

panhandle: Stop people on street and ask for food or money; accost

persnickety: fussy about small details; petty—even worse than perfectionist

pigheaded: Stupidly stubborn (pigheaded resistance)

pipsqueak: A much disliked small or unimportant person; a twerp

rabble-rouser: To appeal to emotions, prejudices to create violent action

rambunctious: Uncontrollably exuberant

razzle-dazzle: Complex maneuver/display to confuse, impress an opponent (sports)

razzmatazz: Double talk

rigmarole: Unnecessary, confusing, elaborate, complicated (foolish) procedure

riffraff: Worthless, disreputable, "trashy" person

rinky dink: Shoddy, cheap, worn out

rue: Regret; feel sorrowful (He will rue the day that he crossed me.)

scuttlebutt: Rumor, gossip

shenanigans: Mere mischief, prankishness, or involving deceit, trickery

shilly-shally: To show indecision, vacillation (It was shilly-shally on his part.)

slipshod: Often followed by the word "manner"; sloppy, careless

smack-dab: Directly, squarely in the middle

spring chicken: A young person (He's no spring chicken.)

teetotaller: Does not participate; especially a non-alcoholic drinker

topsy-turvy: Upside down, in disarray

tommyrot: Nonsense, balderdash, foolishness

twerp: Unimportant, despised person

twit: Insignificant or bothersome person (other meanings, too)

urn: Vase, vessel that holds cremated ashes (note coffee urn, too)

vat: Large vessel, tank to hold liquid (for storing)

voodoo: Magic charm; spells to hurt or get one's way

weasel out: Being sly, cunning, sneaky to get out of a commitment

wheeler-dealer: Slick, shrewd operator in business or politics

whippersnapper: Young (ignorant) know-it-all (and insignificant person)

whoopdedoo: Big deal [whoop = loud yell] of jubilation

willy-nilly: In a disorganized or unplanned manner, sloppily

wince: To slightly draw back in pain or embarrassment with a grimace

wingding: Wild, lively party

zilch: Zero

There is a mountain of books to play around with words; let me just mention a few: *Heavens to Betsy!* and *Hog on Ice* and *Horsefeathers,* all by Charles E. Funk. The following vocabulary game is fun, too—and it's worth the price of this book, alone.

An Original Vocabulary-Building Game

DECISION: Synonym, Antonym, Homonym

[purple]   [red]   [green]   [blue]

DECISION: Synonym, Antonym, Homonym is a categorizing/thinking and vocabulary-building game. It is as much one as the other. Seeing relationships (classifying, categorizing), though a necessary foundation skill for inferencing, deducing (reading), outlining, and writing, is too often drudgery for many students—because the activities to teach this skill do not generate enough interest within the students. *DECISION*, on the other hand, is a stimulating social and academic experience via small-group interaction. The students enjoy the complications of the game with its penalties and benefits

On the other side of the coin, so to speak, to *DECISION* being a thinking game, is its ability to enhance vocabulary. There are programs and printed matter on the market dealing with this area, but in almost every case they dictate to the teacher the vocabulary to be learned. This is pedagogically inefficient, often overwhelming both the teacher and the students—let alone boring them both. And what is so sacrosanct about the particular list of words such programs use?

DECISION, on the other hand, meets the vocabulary needs of the teacher and student; vocabulary the students need to have a working knowledge of because the words are germane to classroom study—whether words that help beginning reading or strengthen math or geography concepts, for instance.

There are few "educational" games that students love to take home to play. *DECISION: Synonym, Antonym, Homonym* is one of them! *DECISION* proves that words can be fun; words that you can include—from basic phonics (although there's an established deck, included herein) to a deck of synonymous words like "polygon/closed curve" (math) and "river bottom/bed" (geography) to antonyms like "hodgepodge/organized"; and how about "perpendicular/parallel" (more math)?

Your students will get smarter the fun way, impress their parents (wow!), and become oh so-o-o educated. (Warning: There are little traps and penalties in *DECISION*, as well as rewards.) So, it will be fun, and if your students happen to start impressing others with their vocabulary ... well, shame on the other students ... and their teacher.

How to Play the Game

1. Each of two to four players is dealt five cards from a well-shuffled pack by the dealer, who is *initially* chosen by the group. Each player's cards must lie face-up for all to see. (A five-card hand/book is to be maintained by each player by drawing from the **"New Cards"** space when necessary.)

2. The dealer also fills each of the board's numbered spaces with a card, face up. Cards not dealt or placed on the board's playing spaces are deposited on the **"New Cards"** space, *face down.*

3. Play begins with the dealer, moves clockwise. The dealer scores the game.

4. If a player chooses, he may match a card *from his hand* with one on the board, in which case he would receive the number value of the exposed board's space plus five points. Or, if two cards *on the board* match, he may choose to collect those cards (especially if the total points would be greater), in which case the value of each card's space will be added.

5. If no match can be made, the player takes one allowed draw from the **"New Cards"** space, and proceeds with his turn.

6. When a player discovers a match in his own or another's hand (which is not allowed), one of these cards must be discarded to the middle of the **"New Cards"** pile and another drawn from its top.

7. Matchable cards will agree in color: synonyms, green; antonyms, red; homonyms, blue. (Players can look at the color-keyed words in the game's title to help them identify the type of relationship/match as antonym, synonym, or homonym.) Matched cards are placed on the **"Played Cards"** space, *face up.*

8. A player is never "out." When a player has matched all his cards, on his/her turn he draws a card from the **"New Cards"** space and tries it, or plays an on-the-

board match. If a match is still not possible, he passes and waits for his/her next turn.

9. Any board spaces emptied because of matching are to be refilled with cards from the **"New Cards"** bank by the dealer. When the **"New Cards"** bank is depleted, the player must use his own card/s to replenish the exposed playing space/s.

10. Any player's match can be challenged. But the challenger will lose ten points to the player if on the backs of the cards the initial letter pairs of each word match. (Only upon a challenge do players refer to the cards' backs.) On the other hand, if the challenger is correct, she/he takes ten points from the player. (The players can be required to ask after each match: "Are there any challenges?")

11. When matching, the player must both show and say aloud the words so other players can see and hear any possible mismatch in order to challenge. The player will identify how the matched words are related by saying, for example, "'Come' and 'go' are antonyms."

12. Players can be required to demonstrate knowledge of homonym differences. This will be decided by the teacher or majority vote of the players at the beginning of play. Any player who matches but incorrectly identifies a homonym's meaning will be penalized ten points.

13. Any player, on his or her turn, can play any single, *unrecognized* match of the *previous* player (whether it was an on-the-board or hand-to-board match)—if that player passed without matching—and still keep his turn. When a player does take advantage of this rule,

the other rules of challenge are still in effect. (But although this player may lose on a challenge, he will still take his schedule turn.)

14. Any unmatchable cards due to unrecognized mismatches are discarded, the game ended, and points tallied.

15. The winner has the highest tally at the end of the game. The player with the lowest score becomes the next game's dealer. (A game takes about twenty minutes.)

How to Introduce the Game

When introducing the game—especially to primary or less skilled students—it may be best not to require the players to identify matches as either synonyms, antonyms, or homonyms unless they are familiar with the concepts. Simply ask (and help) them to look for words that go together because they have any of the following: 1) the same meaning, 2) an opposite meaning, or 3) the same sound. (The meaning of these terms/relationships can be written on the chalkboard or placed elsewhere for reference.) A further help is that only cards (or lettering) of the same color ever match; and that the players can look at the color-keyed terms in the game's title for help in identifying the type of match/relationship.

Likewise, during the *introductory* play of the game, one should merely inform the players of the penalties, but not exact them until about the third game. For example, allow them to refer to the cards' backs to see if they have made a correct match. If a mismatch, the cards will simply be replaced on the board or in the player's hand/book without a penalty. (Not all students will need the introductory three games—which may involve different days—in order to grasp the game's rules.)

Although **DECISION: Synonym, Antonym, Homonym** is reasonably fast-paced once the students are familiar with the rules, the game does demand careful observation and thinking (seeing relationships). Because patience and attention span are especially short in primary and less skilled students, they should be given strong praise for a match and much encouragement for a mismatch or a no-match.

Once the students seem reasonably familiar with the game, all rules can be applied. Once they have enjoyed the game's penalties and benefits, they will be glad to teach others. Eventually, all interested students will learn. (As with any game, alas, a number of pupils will not find **DECISION** to their liking; others will consider it exciting.)

It is also important that during language arts, spelling, or reading periods the whole class will be instructed in the concepts of synonym, antonym, and homonym.

What Skills Are Being Taught?

1. Develops skill at discerning relationships, i.e., classifying.

2. Helps teach/reinforce concepts of homonym, antonym, and synonym—the latter two especially useful in writing.

3. Aids in reinforcing spelling patterns and phonetic combinations. Homonyms reinforce variant combinations for long vowel sounds (ate, eight; road, rode), other vowel digraphs (fault, fought), and some vowel blends (allowed, aloud).

4. Develops/reviews vocabulary. Antonyms and synonyms, especially, can expand vocabulary along lines desired by the teacher, such as terms from subject areas: reading, math, geography, civics, science, social studies; or from local or national vocabulary lists.

Can the Game be Modified?

1. The game can consist entirely of synonym and/or antonyms (see No. 3, below).

2. For the better-skilled students—and/or to foster greater thinking—the cards' word-relationship clue of *colored* cards (or letters) can be eliminated.

3. *DECISION: Synonym, Antonym, Homonym* may have the quality to be two games: *JUNIOR DECISION* for the elementary school student and *DECISION* for junior and high school students as well as adults. The latter would not contain homonyms (may or may not contain color clues), but easily recognized vocabulary to be paired with less frequently used synonyms and antonyms.

DECISION would be a slower paced game (much the speed of Scrabble), but each player might have x number of chances in a game he/she could refer to a dictionary or thesaurus. Additional reference use would exact a penalty of so many points per use.

DECISION would be one additional way an older student could build his or her vocabulary. An important attribute of *DECISION* (and *JUNIOR DECISION*) is that it can improve the poor writing and reading ability of students, which is now a national concern. A better vocabulary would be a step in the right direction, and we teachers are always looking for ways to increase our students' vocabularies.

One motivation for **DECISION** (and **JUNIOR DECISION**) should be that one will make fewer wrong matches the more one plays because one will learn from one's own and others' matches and mismatches; thus an increased vocabulary is inevitable.

The game package should contain a relatively easy introductory set of game cards, one or more advanced sets/decks, and a number of blank decks for the teacher or individual to tailor the game to his/her own needs.

The selection of the synonym and antonym vocabulary should not be random, but chosen from approved or popular lists or based on classroom instruction.

Shorter games can be developed for the primary and less-skilled students (fifteen minutes); longer ones for others (thirty minutes to one hour.

An Introductory Deck

Synonyms: [green]	chief, leader / pie, food / by, near / suit, clothes / coin, money / haul, carry / saw, cut / small, little / fur, hair
Antonyms: [red]	play, work / early, late / me, you / cold, hot / out, in / now, later / boy, girl / hard, soft / north, south / good, bad / get, give / sick, well
Homonyms: [blue]	ate, eight / meet, meat / write, right / rode, road / know, no / blue, blew

Each game will not necessarily have the same total number of cards or the same ratio of types of words. And some homonyms may be repeated in successively numbered games/decks.

The following sounds (and more) are represented in "Game 1"—future games/decks do not have to be based upon such a representation of sound:

ā:	a + e, ai, ay, ei	er:	ir, er, ur
ē:	ea, ee, ie, -y, -e	â:	ar
ī:	i + e, igh, ie, I	or:	or
ō:	o + e, oa, ow, -o	ă	
ū:	ue, ew, oo, ui	ě	
ou:	ou, ow	ĭ	
oi:	oi, oy	ŏ	
ô:	au, ou, aw, of, or, al	ŭ	

The game's cards could be used in phonics lessons to establish the words as sight vocabulary as well as to show their meaning relationships.

Facsimile of a Deck's Title Card—Follow Color Code

DECISION:

Synonym
Antonym
Homonym

(Board and cards should be laminated oaktag and letters should follow color code)

Decision:			
Synonym, Antonym, Homonym ©James T. Charnock			
8			3
1			7
5			9
10			2
4			6
New Cards		**Played Cards**	

Needless to say, you will have to enlarge this playing board via a commercial photocopier or by hand on large plain or appropriately colored oaktag. Once drawn, it should be commercially laminated on both sides—as with the cards. Without lamination, the game will soon be in ruin. Follow the color codes for the game title (bold purple), synonyms (bold green), antonyms (bold red), and homonyms (bold blue) for all letters. The numbers and lines could be in black. Be sure to make the card spaces larger than the 2-by-3.5-inch cards so the cards can easily fit into the spaces

fur S	**hair** S
1 f/h	1 f/h
you A	**me** A
1 y/m	1 y/m
no H	**know** H
1 n/k	1 n/k

<u>Synonyms</u>: Green cards or lettering
<u>Antonyms</u>: Red cards or lettering
<u>Homonyms</u>: Blue cards or lettering

The cards' backs are numbered to identify the set—helps when cards get misplaced, too. The card back also identifies the first letter of the matching words—for challenging purposes.

Please note that the small **S, A,** or **H** on each card's lower front left should be eliminated for all but the introductory decks of cards.

Chapter 16

Assaying the Essay

You *won't* find onerous definitions or strictly defined parameters in this chapter. You *will* find simple examples you can use with your students. Call these "starters," if you wish; we'll leave the minute details of such writing where it belongs—in upper high school or beginning college. (An aside: Did you know that some of the best writers did not take a course in writing?)

Eliminating Frustration

Here's a story to justify my approach in this chapter—and indeed this book. When I was in teacher college I took a course called "How to Teach English in Elementary School." Near the end of this course the professor explained that we students would have to put together a term paper. We grumbled, but that was typical.

Then, she described in detail what she wanted in the content, the approach we were to take, and so on. Hands shot up like a new patch of weeds. We could not fully understand what she was after in spite of her exasperated and repetitious attempts to explain. A good portion of our course grade rested on doing well with this project and we wanted to get it right; we were anxious. The professor eventually discovered she couldn't satisfy our appetite for clarity, so she simply ended the "discussion" and ordered us to perform the task.

Immediately, after class, quite a number of us remained in the room to seek a solution to our problem of incomprehensibility. We finally concluded the professor was incompetent and decided to complain to her superior. It was our misfortune to discover she *was* the superior: fully tenured and, apparently, highly regarded—or, at least, no one would discuss the matter with us.

So, we had to come up with another idea. Our "committee" would meet with the whole class, rather secretly, and appoint a person to speak for the whole class at the next class period. That happened, but the professor was determined to not be pushed around by students.

Luckily, our spokesperson thought of a possible, brilliant idea. She asked the professor whether or not she had required this assignment of former students. The answer was in the affirmative. Next, the professor was asked if she had any such papers and could she bring these in for us to look at. The professor agreed to do so the next period.

When the time came we eagerly perused the efforts of former students (who hadn't bothered to pick up their term papers) and with great relief said, "We can do *that!*" All it took was a few examples to give us a clear picture of what the professor wanted, but couldn't convey to us with words alone. Enough said? Well ….

More for the Doubters

If you are not quite sure what delineates descriptive, argumentative, narrative, persuasive, expository, and such writing, you won't find elaborate definitions herein. I'm not going to be pedantic and clarify such types of writing, their combinations or variations. (Books and the Internet, especially, have good information on essay writing. They define it, sometimes temporarily confusing the reader with new terms for old ones, and are by-and-large good dictionaries. What they too often don't give you is an example with which you can go with immediately.)

Let me give you an analogy to which you can relate. There are times when we need a thingamajig, but can't, for the life of us, remember what it is called; sometimes, even a description of its looks or use doesn't help another person, either. But when we get to the store, we know where to find it. Oh, yes, it's called an "Allen wrench." Now, knowing this handle—a sort of nomenclature—may have been helpful, but it was not imperative.

I never taught—and certainly never tested—my students in their knowledge of grammar or parsing terminology. Do they really need to know what a preposition, gerund, or adverbial clause is by name when *learning* to write? Absolutely not. What they need is to be able to use or mimic such writing forms effectively, correctly, and, hopefully, creatively. And how do they learn? By examples. That is some of what this chapter will provide you.

I Promised Not to, But …

If you're insecure about this approach—or to let you know I know a thing or two about various types of essay or theme writing—ponder this partial list below, or skip it.

VARIOUS TYPES OF ESSAYS/WRITING SKILLS/ WRITING TECHNIQUES

1. *Comparison and Contrast*: Resemblances and differences—or how the topic interacts with other issues.

2. *Argumentation or Persuasion*: Using authorities, personal experience, facts, statistics, even anticipating contrarian views.

3. *Narration*: Change over time or a personal account.

4. *Description*: Can be physical or spatial.

5. *Cause and Effect*: Something happened; then this result happened.

6. *Analytical* : Same as Argumentative.

7. *Chronological*: Can be same as narration.

8. *Climatic*: In order of importance, but can also apply to one or more of the above.

9. *Personal Essay*: Same as narration and what the author thinks.

10. *Inductive and deductive*: Wow, see Chapter 1.

I'm sure reading the above has not made you any happier. So, let me follow with a few examples of student writings—admittedly fledging writers in junior high. Mind you, only a few examples follow. Hopefully, enough to whet your appetite.

EXAMPLES OF INFORMATIVE WRITING

"Washing and Diapering the Baby" *(or "Hold Still, Kid")*

By N.I.

In the morning, parents expect you to help wash, diaper, and dress the baby—as though you don't need time to dress yourself for school or work. The first thing to do is to get lotion, powder, a diaper, and some clean clothes. Next, wash the baby in lukewarm or room temperature water, making sure to wash all the important parts. After drying the baby, put on the lotion and powder, then put the diaper on. Lastly, put on the clothes—which is easier said than done because when you want the baby to go one way it goes the other. So, everything I have written is easier said than done because babies don't cooperate.

"How to Go about Doing the Laundry"

By N.P.

The first thing you have to do when doing the laundry is to separate the clothes that have color from the ones that are white. You have to do this because if you put them together in one washer the colors will go onto the white clothes. (You wouldn't want that; would you?) Also, look at the label of the clothing to see if it says to wash in cold water. Or else the clothing will shrink or lose its color if you put it in hot or very warm water. You have to separate the clothes that need to be washed in cold water, too. So, I guess, you need three washing machines if it is a small load—or three washes.

After you are done with all that trouble, you then put the detergent in. I recommend using Tide; it is pretty good. But use whatever you think is best. Remember to put bleach in with the white clothes. (You want them nice and white, don't you?)

After the washer is done, you just put your clothes in the dryer. But be sure to check the label of the clothing to see if it can be dried in this way. If not you have to hang the washing up to dry. It may shrink by putting it in the dryer.

After that, you are finally done! You now know how to do the laundry. (Was that fun or what?)

"How to Write Punishment Papers for Mr. Charnock"

By Y.T.

As you know, Mr. Charnock does not fool around with punishment writing. I believe it is a hobby since he has given it to some hundreds of people (exaggeration?). But I made it fun and pacified Mr. Charnock's crave for such papers. Writing a sentence such as "I must not run my mouth in class" contains too many words. So, use two pens (right?). But how? Hold two pens in your hand, side-by-side with, or parallel to, each other so that the pens are both on different lines. Then start writing down or across. Two words are written at the same time, making the task twice as fast. (But don't let Mr. Charnock find out.) Have fun!

EXAMPLES OF DESCRIPTIVE WRITING

"My School"

By C.T.

My school is a two-story brick building with a paved yard cracked and crumbled from thousands of feet that have trampled across it.

Inside, paint is peeling from the dirty walls and ceilings which look as if no one has bothered with in thirty years.

In most of the bathrooms, odors emanate like sulfur from the toilets. The bathroom floors are wet—not because of water, but because of urine. The toilets are dry and filled with soda cans and other debris.

On cold winter days the building is bearable, but on hot days even the devil could mistake the place for hell. It is stifling and the lack of air conditioning doesn't help. Adding to the discomfort of the stuffy classrooms is the smell of sweat that's enough to make one faint.

"My Block"

By Y.T.

At the corner of my block is a half-burnt, abandoned house with shattered, empty windows. It seems as if nature has taken control of the land beneath its foundation because the building tilts a little southward and has roots, plants, grass, and animals that dwell in its dingy, cramped insides.

The burnt side has the odor of ash, smoke, and some poor animal that was burned and killed in the path of the deadly, unforgiving fire that took control of the one side.

One thing that stands out is the basement … in no better condition. Large insects of every description inhabit the rusty, sticky, damp walls. Hugging one wall is a large pile of sand (or is it?) with a foul odor. The floor is cracked, chipped, and is otherwise suffering from anything that can happen to a floor. And sticking out from the cracks are the roots of weeds that have died in these unlivable conditions.

"Sunset at the Ocean"

By T.

The cloudless sky is a deep, dark, sea red mixed with blue and pink. The orange-red sun is burning brightly against the beautiful horizon. Black and white seagulls are flying gracefully all around. The ocean is a cerulean blue except where the horizon near the sun is a reflection of red-orange. The waves are calm, almost still: only a breeze is making the waves move. The salty air is warm and the disintegrated sand is still hot from the afternoon sun. Only a few people are out walking on the beach.

EXAMPLES OF COMPARISON WRITING

"My Parents"

By N.P.

My mom and dad are very much alike. They are both generous and caring because they like to help people out. They are both funny and weird and clever. And they expect me and my brother and sister to be smart and successful in the future.

My mom and dad can also be very different. My dad wants things done gradually, while my mom wants things done quickly. My dad doesn't like arguing, my mom gets her point across right away. My dad can be lazy, my mom energetic. My dad jokes a lot, my mom is more serious. My dad doesn't value people's opinions, my mom sometimes does. My dad doesn't worry about much, my mom is a nail biter.

They are both more different than they are similar. This proves that opposites do attract. Ha.

"Being Different from Most"

By H.L.

There are advantages of being a well-behaved student in class. Being a good student can get you good grades and very far in the future. With a good education, and a positive attitude, many employers would accept you. Being good also keeps you out of trouble. Many people can't control their mouths when a teacher says something smart because of their behavior. They talk back to him/her, trying to be even smarter or funnier. You would have respect from a teacher if you would be kind to him/her.

There are also some disadvantages of being well behaved. Bullies may pick on you just because you're smart and you don't get into trouble.

It is better to be a good student than a disturbance because what you are now may determine your later life.

"Being a Loner"

By Anonymous

When I work alone, I do better work because there is nobody to bother me and keep me back. When I am put with a group to do class work, I always have to help the rest of them, and I wind up doing most of the work. There's never anyone of my classmates who can help ME because I'M ALWAYS NUMBER ONE in every class I was ever in. I also receive all the credit I deserve when I am alone as opposed to sharing all the credit with a group when I did all the work.

Sometimes, it gets a little lonely, especially when everybody else is doing something with somebody. And if I get in trouble, like a fight, there's no one to back me up. There's no one with which to play games, watch TV and movies. I always have to play by myself or watch TV all by myself.

But, all in all, I prefer being alone.

EXAMPLE OF ARGUMENTATIVE WRITING

"The All-Year School"

By Y.T.

There are many things that are good about an all-year school. The students will learn more in a year's time and move into the next grade faster. This will allow them to get certain jobs at a younger age than usual. And, in the summer, places such as malls, beaches, and other recreational areas won't be very crowded with the usual number of kids—they'll be in school.

There are also many things that are bad about an all-year school. When the weather is hot in the summer the students will be restless, sweaty, and exhausted (especially if there is no air conditioning). This will make it easier to pass different diseases and make it hard for students to concentrate; their concentration will gradually wear down. In this situation students will also behave differently.

Personally, I would never go to an all-year school.

Chapter 17

Experts: Becoming a True Researcher

This chapter is not last because it is of least importance, but because it is a necessary conclusion to previous ideas. "Research" (or information gathering) often sounds boring or pretentious, but with this approach it is exacting, enjoyable, and within the reach of middle and high school students. Like the creator, Mr. Chrisco (see acknowledgements page), I and others have classroom tested "Experts" and found it to be a most effective, flexible learning and assessment tool for one's year of teaching and student learning. By comparison, this may be a more demanding chapter, but will also be a cooperative venture with your students, one-by-one and with each other, and even their parents. Needless to say, it is an appropriate ending to the rest of the book's teaching of language arts and writing.

At the end of this chapter you will find forms that list the rationales for *Experts* ("Why the *Experts* Approach?"—which can be sent to parents), a guideline sheet for the student ("The Secret to Success in *Experts*"), an informative letter to parents, and the "*Experts* Progress Sheet" that keeps the student on track.

First, I am going to share with you what you should do before you set your students loose on their own formal research effort. This approach, *Experts*, is not written in stone; modify it as you wish. You can do a whole-class research project based on the model first, and when your students are ready to start they can work singly or in pairs or triads.

Choosing Topic

With the idea that learning is best enjoyed and most successful when it is as personal as possible, the students can be shown the following (or your) list of topics as a mere example of the range of possibilities for their research projects:

Aerobics	Peanuts (the plant)
Astrology	Pretzels
Ballet	Outer space
Billiards	Pollution (water, etc.)
Child abuse	Science fiction
Ecology	Solar power
An ethnic group	Street cars/trolleys
A foreign country	Tailoring
The history of hockey	Training animals (dog, cat)
A hobby	Thunder
Ice cream	Toilets
Gypsies	Waterbeds
Local history	Wrestling
Moles	Doll houses

By way of introduction, you can relate the following:

The moles paper, for example, was written by a young man who had found the surrounding yard inhabited by moles. After several unsuccessful attempts to drive the animals off, the young man decided to use the research paper assignment as an opportunity to find out where the little buggers came from, how they lived, and how he might get rid of them.

Besides the information collected from the usual sources, the student talked with a gardener and the local hardware store pest-control "expert." Also, the inclusion of a brief summary of the student's personal experience with the animal made for a lively, interesting, and humorous opening for the paper (and presentation). This was an excellent example of a seemingly dull topic made more interesting by the honest and personal interest the researcher had in the subject from the beginning.

Brainstorming

Brainstorming is a problem-solving technique that accepts, without criticism or immediate evaluation, the spontaneous ideas from individual group members. After a cutoff time (and some prefer, also, a length of time—a day or two), a non-critical vote on which idea(s) to keep can be taken. Some allow evaluative statements to be made about the ideas at this time.

The purpose of brainstorming is to discover how much we already know and to bring into consciousness what we want to know to solve the problem or answer the question(s).

Suppose a twosome chose "Gypsies" as their research inter-est. This is much too general, though an acceptable beginning. But by brainstorming questions (who, what, why, where, when, how), the possible aspects of the topic are realized. For example, some of the following questions may come to mind:

1. Who are the Gypsies?	7. What do they look like?
2. Where do they live?	8. How long have they been around?
3. How do they live?	9. What do others think of them?
4. What do they do?	10. Why are they different?
5. How are they different?	11. Which Gypsies are famous?
6. What do they believe?	

Although some of the above questions may be redundant, this will be discovered later, not while initially racking one's brain. Often, some questions will make more sense than others; and, of course, other questions could be asked.

The partners will next pick one of the above questions that most interest them and continue the procedure of brainstorm-ing. Suppose, again, the twosome decides to deal with "How are Gypsies different?" The following questions could be prompted by this inquiry:

1. Do they dress differently?	4. Their beliefs about others?
2. Is their food different?	5. Their looks (features)?
3. Their religion?	

The answer to some of these questions will cancel out certain questions from the previous list. With some topics this latter group of questions may constitute the entire focus of the research; otherwise it will simply serve as a means to "get into" the paper—to analyze and discover the topic.

Outlining

There are two reasons for outlining. One is for organizing a composition to be written or spoken. The other is to make a skeletal picture of an oral or written composition already completed—such as an article, interview, or speech/lecture.

Outlining can be chronological or topical. The latter requires more cognitive effort.

As important as outlining is in helping students discover or create the relation of one idea to another, it should be remembered that some of the best writers use outlines and some do not. Others use them only sometimes. Some use them often. The point is that it is not always essential to outline before getting an organized piece of writing. Nor is a finished, well-written piece of writing always easily reducible to an outline.

Outlining requires analyzing. And therein lies its value for constructing a well thought-out project or reflecting its structured ideas. It is reasonable to assume that this struggle to order thought may foster better writing and better comprehension.

Nevertheless, students can become good outliners (planners) and remain poor writers. Some can write well, but pre-outline poorly. Some persons can, to repeat, simply write in an organized fashion if they know *what* they want to say—though they will discover just *how* they want to say it as they write.

An essential element in writing a piece that makes sense or "feels right" to the author is his or her own interest in the message. If writers are inspired they will do better. Therefore, keep in mind that teaching outlining without ever allowing for student personal interest will be an uphill task.

Topical outlining, especially, is based on seeing relationships. You may wish to start with categorizing activities using objects or words. Let the students discover how the objects or words can be grouped or listed. There are many commercially prepared materials in this area. But also refer to this book's chapter on "Paragraphing and Compositions—a Step-by-Step Approach."

Summarizing

Summarizing a paragraph, article, interview, or presentation means to restate the most important points—in one's own words. This restatement can be initially made in note-taking form (see elsewhere) or outline form (which can be called a form of note taking, too). This summary may then be reflected in a fuller composition.

Before students can summarize they must comprehend the source of the information. If they do understand what they are reading, seeing, or hearing (and summarizing practice should eventually include all three), then the only skill to learn is how to generalize the information into a condensed version.

Teachers involve students in summarizing, to some extent, when they ask them to state the main idea (or choose it among several listed). A simple form of this skill is practiced when students paraphrase (restate) a sentence, keeping the essence of the original. When students are expected to support a conclusion they have drawn by providing evidence, this entails recognition of subordinate ideas and seeing relationships—a skill needed in summarizing as well as outlining.

Have the students provide several slang expressions to be written on the board, such as: He's a cool cat; That's a "bad" car; He hit a single. The students will now translate these into language anyone might understand. (There may be some debate about the exact translation of slang expressions.)

This next activity may seem too easy, but some students find it difficult. Write a sentence with two or more clauses or phrases and have the students write it differently, but keep the essence of its meaning.

Another approach is to use an informational, nonfiction, interesting short article easily read by the students. Focus attention on each paragraph, then the entire article. Determine with the class what each paragraph (or a unit of them) is about, its main points, then the subordinate or related details. When the paragraphs are analyzed thusly, focus on the entire article. (As has been covered elsewhere, this is very similar to the procedure used in outlining, which some consider desirable as a preliminary skill to summarizing. But others may find summarizing practice to help outlining.)

The result of this focusing will be a written statement—a paraphrase—of the paragraph's or article's meaning: a statement of its main idea(s), the gist of the information.

It will take several sessions (at least five) before most students will even begin to do a reasonably accurate job of summarizing.

It is good to keep in mind that summarizing is not alien to the students. They are constantly restating and giving brief oral accounts of events in their lives: a film, a fight, gossip—to mention a few.

Note Taking

We make notes to later write a paper, give a presentation, or use as a resource for study. But note taking is near the top of a hierarchy of skills, and requires the use of prerequisite competence and knowledge.

Prerequisites

In order to take notes one must be able to outline (if that is the type of notes one will make) and to summarize. To do these efficiently one must know how to recognize what information is important enough to record (in one's own words—apart from quotes); and, for outlining, especially, to see parallel and sequential relationships among the ideas presented. And to go back even further, practice in categorizing (objects then words) will foster the idea of relationships needed for outlining. Likewise inherent in summarizing is the recognition of main and subordinate points. All this reflects comprehension, intellectual maturity, and/or interest. Thus, separating the components of a basic study, and research skill, such as note taking, is not easy.

Because note taking relies upon comprehension of the reading material (of course, oral presentations are germane, too) it is best to use reading matter easy for most students, informational (nonfiction) in nature, and interesting. (Two good sources of appropriate short articles are *Highlights for Children* and *Cricket Magazine*—both juvenile magazines. And if you re dealing with high school students still keep it easy.)

A reading selection at a challenging, even average, level of difficulty, that's uninteresting, just adds to the effort of teaching and learning note taking. Let the taking of notes be the students' only challenge. In other words, the students' preparation-practice should amount to a simple working model of what they will do in the real situation with more difficult material. Don't look upon this instruction as "dumbing down" to students.

When we take notes we are finding answers to certain questions we have come to the resource with or that have come into consciousness while searching, listening, or observing. Often we run across information that had not previously occurred to us as important. Most likely our immediate purpose is to get the main and subordinate ideas of a particular article or interview, but our ultimate goal may be to use this accurately-gathered information to add detail to a related topic.

Dealing with Comprehension

Remember that *accurate* note taking involves an adequate understanding of the resource. *Efficient* note taking demands confidence in writing in abbreviated form.

Place the title of an article on the board. Have the students predict what is in the article or what questions the article will answer—or should answer. Write their questions—in note-taking form—on the board. Have them read the article, then record their answers to the questions for them on the board—always using note-taking form.

In later sessions, have threesomes work together in the above procedure. This will increase individual participation, alertness, and learning. The session should end with group representatives sharing their group's questions, answers, and/or note taking with the entire class. (Of course, if you have a difficult class, disciplinary-wise, have the students work independently.)

As a variation of the above, have the students make educated guesses as to the answers to the questions before they read the article. Afterward they can compare their guesses with what they have discovered.

After the above practice, give each student the same short article to silently read and take notes on all or a portion of it. Next, pairs or threesomes meet to compare the essence of their notes: Miss the main ideas? Too many details? Too few details? Too much verbatim copying? They should come to a consensus. Next, meet with the whole class and have a person from each group volunteer the group's agreed-upon notes for portions of the article. Others can react to these notes. (You may wish to review the techniques for summarizing included previously.)

Please note that it may take at least several sessions (five or more) before most of the students will feel confident enough to go it alone with note taking. Never have the students take notes just to keep in practice—I've heard of a lot of that! Instead, provide them with personal, realistic assignments that will rely upon the use of the new and developing skill.

The hardest part for the students may be learning what information to record out of the great quantity an article contains. The easiest way for the students to determine this is to know what they are looking for; that is, they must have formed some questions beforehand or are dealing with some preconceived ideas. Apart from this the students may "simply" record the main and important subordinate ideas. If students have trouble with the latter, their difficulty is comprehension, most likely, not note taking. The failure to comprehend can be the result of many things, but it is not pertinent to a discussion of note taking that assumes comprehension. (Nevertheless, the previous techniques of pre-reading questioning and predicting can help students understand the information better and perhaps to the extent of getting correct answers to their questions.)

Dealing with the Mechanics

Give the students practice, as individuals and groups, in using abbreviated syntax (using only important words) by having them rewrite your full sentences and by writing telegrams where they must get across a given message with the least number of words. The latter can be competitive fun.

Interviewing

There is a previous chapter on interviewing, but that is not as closely related to a research report.

An interview adds interest to a report because it gives a personal viewpoint. It enlivens the task of information gathering and helps the researcher connect outside his or her own select group. From the standpoint of skill building, the interviewer, by the technique of probing, with some evaluating and conclusion drawing, is practicing a process of inquiry—a skill necessary in any research project.

Teaching Techniques

You may wish to give the students practice in interviewing (see related previous chapter) before they attempt the important one for their project. This "dry run" is called "partnership interviewing," in which the members of a twosome interview each other. The pairing of students can be by their choice, random drawing, or teacher direction.

Although this interview is in preparation for a later one, it is important. Each student will have a personal stake in what is being written about him or her. There is the pleasure and apprehension of being an audience. Students will take these interviews seriously because the interviews will be read before the class. Both partners, though, should consent beforehand; that is, they should work on the drafts until they are satisfied enough to consent.

The immediate objective of these interviews is for each partner to get to know, to reveal, each other well. They will prepare questions beforehand of a concrete nature (such as "What places have you lived?") and move on with open-ended, abstract questions as "How do you feel about abortion?" (assuming an older teenager). The partners will try to discover their similarities and differences and draw out the other's particular area of interest or an issue about which she or he has strong feelings.

While the students are taking turns interviewing each other (asking prepared and spontaneous questions), they are recording the answers in note-taking form (see appropriate section of this chapter). After the notes are compiled, the students write their draft without each other's aid. Next, the partners exchange papers to comment on their accuracy, strengths, and weaknesses. The final draft should be agreed upon by both. If it should happen that both cannot agree, then no oral presentation of it should be given. Nevertheless, all final drafts must be handed in.

The "Real" Interview

The interview may be with an acquaintance or a complete stranger. It may take place face-to-face in the community or by long-distance telephone or e-mail. (A face-to-face meeting is much preferred—and you may require it—since long-distance communication, for the purpose of this book, should involve letter writing or e-mailing.)

The students (partners) should not set up the interview until it has been prepared. Some reading on the subject (person, vocation, or topic) should have been done, at least, if possible. Of course, questions should be readied. The interviewee should be told the reason for, or the focus of, the interview, an appointment made, and a time limit set. If the interviewee's job is of importance, then an on-the-job meeting is desirable.

Note taking is covered elsewhere, but the students should be made aware of the importance of sitting down immediately after the interview to write the notes out at length—or at the very least make them legible. A tape recorder may be of use unless it makes the students or subject uncomfortable. Regardless, the latter's permission for its use should be obtained beforehand.

The greatest concern may be in determining what to talk about. This is why questions are prepared. Some questions will arise out of the students' background reading. Others will result in the need to ask for elaboration during the interview. And, quite often, the interviewee helps the students along.

Sometimes the focus of a project is the interviewee, alone. At other times this individual is a means to an end—part of the information-gathering process about a topic in which the interviewee has personal knowledge or expertise. Regardless, in forming questions it may be useful to divide them into the two or three following groups:

1. Establish the person's authority and his or her relationship with the chosen topic. For example, if the subject is a kite maker, the students should find out how long the person has been in business, how well the kites sell, how big the company is by comparison. (Depending on the topic, such information may or may not be crucial.)

2. Get detailed information about the subject's personal life related to the topic. Even if the focus of the interview is the interviewee, it is still about the person as a singer or reporter, for example. In other words, questions about the history of his or her interests as well as the history of the topic or business (above) is appropriate. This information will add interest and real life to the finished product.

3. Depending on the topic, it will be insightful to get the person to express feelings about problems related to his or her field, and their history and solution.

Finding Interview Subjects (People)

If students do not know who to interview, they can consult others for direction. A librarian may provide references listing organizations dealing with the topic of choice. A local expert may be found using the Internet. The public library has hard copy and electronic (Info Trac) databases. If the topic is child abuse, for example, organizations can be found dealing with this. Or it may be that information about child abuse may be gained from an interview about runaways. The students may be able to meet with a social worker or juvenile division police officer.

Writing Up the Interview

The students should observe the subject being interviewed, not just record the message. The person's looks, movements, gestures, side stories, and opinions should be noted. This description gives the subject a sense of character, a realness.

The easiest format in which to present a written interview is the verbatim (but edited) conversation:

Dunn: Did you know Roger Stauback?

Hinton: Yes, I did. We were ...

The more challenging approach is to write a narrative describing the interaction between the subject and the interviewers, and the setting of the action. The setting can be established in the introduction to the written piece. If the setting changes, this can be mentioned. One's own feelings before, during, and after the meeting are legitimate to include as part of the setting.

The following is an example of how one might start an interview:

At 1:15 I turned into the driveway and was promptly greeted by two German Shepherds barking furiously. However, by the time I had stopped the car, they were both standing on their hind legs looking in the driver's window and wagging their tails. This was my welcome to the home of Beth-Anne Chard, who greeted me at the door and warmly accepted me into her home.

The following paragraph from an interview with a child in a reform school shows how the writer tried to convey a sense of character:

We sat down on the floor in the hall, and she pulled a cigarette out of her tiny purse and lit it. Deciding that the best choice would be to ignore it, I began by asking her why she had to go to court in the first place. "Shoplifting" was her answer and given with a really "cute" smile. I am sure that the look on my face belied my answer of "Oh, yeah," I was mortified. She looked very young, so I asked her how old she was. She told me that she was eleven years old and that she had done about everything, including stabbing her cat with a fork.

Letter Writing

Letter writing or e-mailing, for the purpose of this project, is to ask questions (i.e., interview by letter) and to send thanks. The former should be written after the students have read something on the topic chosen, have found out as much as possible about the interviewee beforehand, and, perhaps, had practice in partnership interviewing (see that chapter in this book). Time is of essence, though, so the letter of inquiry may not be possible.

Apart from the composition skills, the mechanics of the letter (and envelope) format is all that needs to be pointed out to the students. Hanging a poster of a short letter and envelope will help serve this purpose. If more practice is needed beyond that provided in the appropriate chapter in this book, there are many commercial materials available.

On the following pages you will see the actual *Experts* program forms. The first explains why *Experts* is so beneficial: "Why the Experts Approach?" The next form is a letter to send to parents telling them of their child's research decision and how they may help—I would also include the preceding form for their edification. Thirdly is the *"Experts* Reference Sheet," the foundation (required resources) of the student's investigation. Then, fourthly, the student gets a necessary pep talk in "The Secret to Success in *Experts.*" Finally comes the *"Experts* Progress Sheet," which keeps the student, parent, and teacher informed of the progress of the research; the blocks have to be initialed by the teacher as the student completes them (and the teacher will most likely want to see, correct, and evaluate most of these items).

WHY THE *EXPERTS* APPROACH?

(Purposely Redundant)

1. Students learn to see world as a resource.

2. Students motivate themselves and each other.

3. There is emphasis on both process and product.

4. There is plenty of interesting content.

5. Reaches all levels of discourse.

6. Meets kids where they are.

7. Lets children know they have something to share.

8. Helps them see their uniqueness.

9. Lets kids invest themselves in learning.

10. Helps students manage time.

11. Builds responsibility for own learning.

12. Allows students to work at a variety of levels.

13. Allows flexible use of time.

14. Encourages students to work with each other.

15. Students teach each other.

16. Encourages use of a variety of media.

17. Gives guidelines, directions, and limits.

18. Helps students understand teaching and learning processes.

19. Involves parents (and/or family members).

20. Is preparation for research—or for harder research.

21. Students experience public speaking.

22. Sets high standards of study.

23. Is holistic.

24. Kids build on their strengths.

25. Kids learn to listen to each other.

26. They learn to ask good questions.

27. Builds on experience: can see what they know and don't know.

28. Students learn how to learn.

29. Is applicable to more than one subject area.

30. Is suitable for students functioning at grade five and above.

Dear Parents:

As a study assignment, the students in my class have chosen areas of learning that are of interest to them. Certain students will elect to work alone; others will prefer a partner. Some will already know a great deal about their topic from past experience, while the selection for others will simply be of present interest. Regardless of past knowledge, they will have to become "experts" in the area selected in order to make a presentation that is of interest to fellow students.

But help may be necessary along the way. And that is why this letter is coming to you. A guide in the form of a check-off progress sheet has been provided each student, but your help in preparing some individual assignments may be needed, such as: forming good questions; how to find and use certain reference materials; proper letter writing; art work; speech/presentation practice; Internet research; and so on.

As much help as possible will be given at school. But with everyone or another doing a different project (and other studies to cover throughout the day), there will not be enough school time or energy to give the fullest attention to each project. Besides, it is rather nice (even important) that a parent can become involved with a son's or daughter's learning.

Please keep in mind, though, if and when your son or daughter calls upon you to help, you are to play the part of a tutor or consultant—not a doer of the assignment. Otherwise, my student will learn little about how to gather information and put together a presentation on his or her own.

Even if you do not have much time or your son or daughter finds it easier to do the project entirely alone or with a student partner, you can still check to see if the work is progressing toward the presentation date.

Here is what the students will learn something about in this *Experts* or research and information-gathering project:

- Note taking
- Composing (letter writing, organizing a written report, and oral presentation)
- Translating knowledge into a graph or other visual media
- Interviewing
- Public speaking
- Using reference materials
- Learning a procedure for future projects: term papers, research, presentations

----

(Please return)

Students sometimes fail to deliver this information to their parents. Therefore, to inform me that you have received this, would you please sign this tear sheet and have it returned soon? Thank you.

Parent's signature: _____

THE SECRET TO SUCCESS IN *EXPERTS*

You've picked your topic. You know your presentation date. Now what?

Now it is time to work. You will have time in class, but that won't be enough. You may have to spend twenty to forty minutes nearly daily working on this project at home or elsewhere.

Some suggestions

Find a place that is quiet where you won't be disturbed. If you leave materials at home, leave them in a safe place. Safe from babies, pets, and house-cleaning family members.

Placing your work in a folder or large envelope is a good idea.

You can involve your parents and others: a partner, family members, librarians, and classmates. It is not cheating to have others help you. They possess some knowledge and skills you don't have. But it is cheating to let them do more than help. Remember, *you* have to give the presentation, so *you* have to know your stuff. (Even if you don't involve your parents, they may check on the progress of your project.)

Keep in mind

You have a *lot* of work, but a *limited* time in which to do it. Time is going to fly—in class and at home. So, plan your time well. Decide which tasks need to be, or can be, done first. Check your progress with your parents and, if you have one, with your partner. Check off or color in completed work on the "*Experts* Progress Sheet."

A surprise for you

You already know a lot. If you are excited you can interest others. The real secret to success in this project is that you have a lot to offer this world and this world has a lot to offer you. Make full use of your life. Always do your best and you will become ... an *expert!*

EXPERT'S PROGRESS SHEET

Name: _____

Topic: _____

Presentation date: _____

(Signatures)

Student: _____

Parent: _____

Teacher: _____

RESEARCH

_____ Topic chosen   _____ Words listed

_____ Topic brainstormed   _____ Words categorized

_____ Questions formed

_____ Partner chosen _____

Phone #: _____

E-mail address: _____

[To teacher: refer to Chapter 1 for listing/categorizing words.]

_____ Source book 1 chosen   _____ Source book 2 chosen

_____ Notes taken (10)   _____ Notes taken (10)

_____ Reference Sheet filled in

___ Reference book chosen   ___ Reference Sheet filled in

___ Notes taken (8)

_____ Magazine 1 chosen   _____ Magazine 2 chosen

_____ Notes taken (6)   _____ Notes taken (6)

_____ Reference Sheet filled in

Local resource person picked (name) _____

_____ Questions drafted (12)   _____ Interview practiced

_____ Questions finalized   _____ Reference Sheet filled in

_____ Interview date set _____   ___ Thank-you note sent

Distant resource person (name) _____

_____ Questions drafted (12)   _____ Letter finalized

_____ Questions finalized   _____ Letter sent: _____

_____ Letter drafted   _____ Reference Sheet filled in

_____ Answer received: _____

_____ Web Site notes taken (4) _____ Web Site notes taken (4)

_____ Project notes completed   _____ Written report drafted

_____ Notes categorized   _____ Written report revised

        _____ Written report finalized

_____ Survey questions drafted   _____ Survey conducted

_____ Questions finalized   _____ Survey graph drafted

        _____ Survey graph finalized

MEDIA

(Art, posters, pictures, slides, film, sound recording, etc.)

1. _____

2. _____

3. _____

4. _____

_____ Media designed   _____ Media finalized

_____ Self evaluation made _____Conference (all material in)

        _____ Road show to other classes (optional)

[The teacher can enlarge these work wheets for students]

EXPERT'S REFERENCE SHEET

Name _____

Partner _____

Topic _____

- **Source book 1** (title) _____

  Author _____ Year pub'd _____

- **Source book 2** (title) _____

  Author _____ Year pub'd_____

- **Reference book** (name)_____

  Volume _____   Pages _____   Date _____

- **Magazine 1** (name) _____   Date _____

  Article title _____

- **Magazine 2** (name) _____   Date _____

  Article title _____

- **Local resource person** _____

- **Distant resource person** _____

  Letter sent on _____   Answer received on _____

- **Web Site 1** researched _____

- **Web Site 2** researched _____

About the Author

James Charnock, M.ED, is a veteran of thirty years of teaching at the elementary and junior high levels, and for most of those years, a certified reading-language arts specialist. In addition to creating educationally oriented market products, for several years he was a feature writer/children's book reviewer for a national reading journal (*The Reading Teacher*) and has served on the editorial board of a national English journal (*Language Arts*).

Former top students have honored him—not once or twice, but four times (less than *two percent* of teachers are so honored *twice*) by placing him in *Who's Who Among America's Teachers*— "The best teachers in America chosen by the best students." He was "*the* teacher who made a difference." He has also been listed in *Who's Who in the East*.

Mr. Charnock has written one other book, *Mt. Horeb: The Little White Schoolhouse on Little Deer Creek,* about the history and memories of one of Maryland's last one-room schoolhouses, where he started his education. The subtitle to this book is *A Brief History of Small Schools and the Sad Story of Consolidation.*

The author lives in a suburb of Philadelphia, where he continues as a freelance writer, often serving as a seminar speaker on the teaching of writing. He also volunteers his time to the local chapter of Habitat for Humanity and teaches an adult course in paper art.

Printed in the United States
40483LVS00006BA/193-210

9 781587 365218